This book is for y

- work with others;

- wish to achieve results;

- want to learn more about yourself and your relationship with others;

- want to lead, not just manage;

- want to anticipate problems before they arise;

- are unsure of what action to take in the situation you are facing;

- are too confident of the action you are going to take and want to explore other options;

- are looking for a creative way out of a sticky situation;

- don't know what to do;

- are in a meeting that is boring you silly and you'd like to move things on by asking incisive questions;

- have team members who just aren't getting it and you need to ask different questions;

- need a challenge;

- find yourself in one of the 47 situations listed in the book and would like to find your way out.

What people are saying about this book...

"It was a delight to read a management book which reflects the true complexity of organisational leadership. This book challenges directors to systematically test their knowledge of how well an organisation is working and their contribution to the organisation by working through 99 questions. The process helps to force innovative thinking into the organisational culture – every non-executive director should buy a copy."

Dr. Dougal Goodman
Chief Executive, The Foundation for Science and Technology

ᔕ

"A thoughtful collection of insights and, even better, penetrating questions for generating your own best insights."

Professor Maury Peiperl
Pro-Vice-Chancellor and
Director of Cranfield School of Management

"The most successful entrepreneurs have an internal framework where they focus on the fundamental truths underlying a problem before devising a solution. This book provides such a framework."

Mike Lynch
Founder, Invoke Capital; Co-Founder, Autonomy Corporation

‫ॐ

"This book provides an excellent concise source of things to think about and things to do in many business situations. A friendly expert on your case!"

Jon Moulton
Founder, Better Capital

‫ॐ

"The book is fascinating. The beauty of it is that it can continue to grow as new situations and new questions arise."

Barry Oshry
Author, *Seeing Systems: Unlocking the Mysteries of Organizational Life*

About THE 7 authors

Gia Campari

Leadership has a greater influence on the overall well-being of an organisation – financial, ethical, place to work – than any other element, and this has become the focus of Gia's work. Gia's experience as a research chemist at the ETH in Zurich, the University of London and in industry, has left a permanent desire for innovation – the constant search for the unexpected, simple solution to organisational issues.

Following an MBA at London Business School, Gia specialised in marketing and business strategy with the silicone valley-based SRI. A Swedish-based boutique consultancy introduced Gia to facilitation, which allowed her to lead culture/performance improvement/change projects for major organisations in Europe and the USA. Gia's interest in creativity led her to introduce creativity to the change process.

Gia founded Signals of Change to help individuals and teams grow through leadership and innovation. Gia has lectured in creativity and leadership at universities in Italy and has served on the board of a software multinational and a manufacturing SME.

g.campari@signalsofchange.com

David Glassman

David has enjoyed a portfolio career with particular emphasis on creativity and its leadership. Increasingly over the last 20 years, David has coached and mentored successful chief executives and entrepreneurs who wished to achieve even more in organisations undergoing rapid change.

After studying chemistry, chartered accountancy, business administration and arbitration, David realised that the key aspects for generating fast and robust growth were the human ones.

David's experience includes roles as a director of quoted and private groups, an independent director appointed by investors, such as Lazards and 3i, and as an investor.

David has been involved in all stages of corporate development, from start-up and turnaround, through fast growth to acquisition and succession, and in firms with a marketing bias in many industry sectors at home and overseas. David has also led turnarounds to deliver speedy returns to profit, cash generation and secure futures.

David was a Visiting Fellow at Cranfield University's School of Management for many years and was a course director on its renowned Business Growth Programmes. David writes, by invitation, on entrepreneurship matters for the *Financial Times*. David was a group chairman in Vistage, the leading membership chief executive organisation and was the honorary treasurer of the Tavistock Institute of Human Relations.

David has worked on numerous charity trustee boards and is currently involved in projects for the Worshipful Company of Management Consultants and the Cranfield Trust. David sits on the council of the Anglo Netherlands Society.

david@glassman.com

Michael Jeans

Michael has held leadership positions ever since his time at the University of Bristol where he was president of Athletic Union (the body responsible for all sport) and Captain of Boats (rowing is the ultimate team sport in his view!).

At KPMG, he rose to be a member of the overall UK board and senior consulting partner before he decided to leave in 1994 to pursue a portfolio career. During his time at KPMG, he was one of a very small group of people drawn from other consulting firms and Harvard that developed Activity Based Costing which flew in the face of traditional accounting wisdom.

He has been the president of two professional institutes (Institute of Management Consultancy and Chartered Institute of Management Accountants) and master of three livery companies (Management Consultants, Haberdashers and Chartered Accountants).

Michael has been the executive chairman of a firm of solicitors (Bevan Brittan), deputy chairman of Gemserv Ltd (a consultancy specialising in utility regulation), and a member of committees of the General Medical Council and General Council of the Bar.

He was awarded an honorary degree by Cranfield University in 1996 and the MBE in 2006.

michael@quagon.co.uk

Marius,

Best wishes

Michael

6

December 2016

Patrick McHugh

Patrick is the chairman and chief executive of Trinity Management Advisers. Trinity is an advisory business founded in 2004 and works with organisations aiming to achieve accelerated performance during change such as implementation of technology, at market entry or during turnaround.

He is the chairman of trustees of La Nuova Musica, a vocal and instrumental ensemble dedicated to the music of the European Renaissance and Baroque, and is honorary secretary of the Foundation for Science and Technology. Formerly he was the chairman of Bell Educational Services Limited providing language education in English for adult students and young learners. Patrick also was a group director of J Sainsbury Plc and a member of the Group Executive Committee responsible for the e-commerce portfolio.

He was the chairman of Taste Network Ltd., a TV channel, the Destination Wine Company, a home delivery wine company, and a non-executive director of GlobalNetXchange, a B2B network. Patrick's career as a management consultant included vice-president with A.T. Kearney, management consultants where he had leadership responsibility for the European Strategic Information Technology Practice and managing partner with Coopers & Lybrand, responsible for the engineering sector of the consulting practice.

Patrick is a co-author of *Business Process Reengineering - BreakPoint Strategies for Market Dominance* (J Wiley & Sons), *The Chain Imperative* (Mercury Books) and *Beyond Business Process Reengineering - Towards the Holonic Enterprise* (J Wiley & Sons).

patrick@thetrinitygroup.co.uk

David Peregrine-Jones

David Peregrine-Jones' lifelong interest in science and philosophy led him to win a scholarship to read Natural Sciences at Cambridge University and subsequently to maintain an ongoing interest in many of the subsequent advances in theoretical physics. Through later work at London Business School, he developed it into related areas such as financial economics, statistical arbitrage, complexity theory and business modelling.

During his IBM career, he held a range of sales and marketing positions, mainly in the finance sector. On leaving IBM, he founded the Torus Business Web Ltd to bring together the best international teams needed to the specific needs of each client engagement. They range from improving the performance of international sales teams to responding to the threats and opportunities arising from the digital disruption of existing sectors such as health. This has led to the emergence of a world-class capability for rapid delivery of powerful business models that provide answers to some of the big questions these changes pose.

David works with a wide range of consultants and business partners across the US, the UK and Asia. He is the chairman of the Richmond Group of Management Consultants, and Master of the Worshipful Company of Management Consultants. He is a trustee of FutureVersity (a charity focused on encouraging children in and around Tower Hamlets to become more employable) and of EISCA (which rescued and then took forward the contents of the former Exeter Boat Museum).

David lives with his partner Caroline in an old Georgian house, close to the River Thames and Hampton Court, conveniently situated for his two favourite sports of Real Tennis and dinghy sailing.

davidpj@torusbw.com

David Shannon

David is the principal and managing director of Oxford Project Management Ltd (OPM), a management consultancy founded in 1988. He studied Natural Science at Oxford University, practiced civil engineering, became a senior management consultant and joined the staff of the World Bank. Since returning to the UK, he has led assignments in such fields as central and local government, chartered institutions and large and small private sector companies. His focus is on helping directors and managers identify and realise opportunities, usually through workshops, process improvements, mentoring and training.

He is active in the Association for Project Management (APM) in which he was a director and deputy chairman and championed the application of governance to project portfolios. He was voted one of the 10 most influential people in Project Management in the UK. His contribution to the profession was recognised by APM with an honorary fellowship.

As well as in the public and private engineering and transport sectors, OPM's experience leading change programmes covers such varied fields as wildlife management in Africa, National Training programmes in Mauritius and, in the UK, legal services, the BBC and the British Standards Institution.

David.Shannon@opmg.co.uk

Benjamin Taylor

 Benjamin is the chief executive of the Public Service Transformation Academy and managing partner of RedQuadrant. He studied philosophy, politics, and economics at Oxford University before becoming co-ordinator of a youth development charity. For seven years, he was adviser to the leader of Hammersmith and Fulham council. That led to a career in PricewaterhouseCoopers and Sector Projects (part of Capita group), where he worked with clients from the Government of Armenia to Birmingham City Council.

He has undertaken voluntary accreditation missions for Youth Business International in Bangladesh, Norway and Dominica. Benjamin is passionate about commissioning, systems thinking, customer-led transformation, lean, and generally thinking about better ways to run and lead organisations. He is an accredited power+systems trainer and lean six sigma black belt. Benjamin is a visiting lecturer in applied systems thinking at Cass Business School, City University, and has lectured at Nottingham Business School and Oxford Said/HEC Paris.

RedQuadrant is a network consultancy working to transform the experience of customers and employees. They design and implement transformation work in services and public services, and build their clients' capacities to help themselves.

benjamin.taylor@redquadrant.com

Please come and visit our website,

www.99essentialquestions.com
and Twitter @99essentialQs

where you can:

- download the Incisive Questioning technique;

- get ideas on how to make the best use of this book;

- order the app;

- order more copies of the book;

- find out about joining our workshops on 'How to ask the questions that really matter!';

- engage through an interactive forum with other readers of the book; and

- contribute to a second edition of the book.

"To raise new questions,
new possibilities,
to regard old problems
from a new angle,
requires creative imagination
and marks real advance in science."

Albert Einstein

Ask the right questions. Make the right decisions.

THE 99 ESSENTIAL BUSINESS QUESTIONS

To take you beyond the obvious management actions

Gia Campari, David Glassman, Michael Jeans,
Patrick McHugh, David Peregrine-Jones,
David Shannon, Benjamin Taylor

Published by
Filament Publishing Ltd
16 Croydon Road, Beddington, Croydon,
Surrey, CR0 4PA, United Kingdom.
Telephone +44 (0)20 8688 2598
www.filamentpublishing.com

ISBN 978-1-910819-89-0

Printed by IngramSpark.

Table of contents

In Broken Images

He is quick, thinking in clear images;
I am slow, thinking in broken images.

He becomes dull, trusting to his clear images;
I become sharp, mistrusting my broken images.

Trusting his images, he assumes their relevance;
Mistrusting my images, I question their relevance.

Assuming their relevance, he assumes the fact;
Questioning their relevance, I question the fact.

When the fact fails him, he questions his senses;
When the fact fails me, I approve my senses.

He continues quick and dull in his clear images;
I continue slow and sharp in my broken images.

He in a new confusion of his understanding;
I in a new understanding of my confusion.

Robert Graves

Preface

You are probably reading this book because you are curious. Or, more likely, because you are in a quandary. You are looking for answers. So this is the right time, at the beginning of the book, to tell you that this book does not contain answers. It contains questions, which will uncover the hidden problems behind most business situations. Once you've uncovered the hidden problems, a solution will be much easier to find. The right questions, and your answers, provide you with the insight to take the right decisions and act in a way which goes beyond the obvious.

This book came about as a result of a series of conversations at the Worshipful Company of Management Consultants, a livery company of the City of London. The seven authors are seasoned management consultants with a collective experience of over 200 years of professional practice. The book grew from our desire to capture our experience of insightful questioning and to package it in a way that would be accessible and useful for practising managers.

Like the practice of management consultancy itself, we have been on a learning journey. Over time, our focus has shifted from solving problems using our expert knowledge, to creating shareable methodologies, to mentoring our clients to help them to develop their own solutions. We now prefer the mentoring approach – it takes longer, but is also much more effective in leaving our clients better off after we have left, as they learn to help themselves. Each of these approaches to consultancy has its own strengths and weaknesses and has its own place, but ultimately each of them relies on the ability to ask the right questions.

Whether you are trying to understand the dynamics that underlie the apparent problem in order to apply the right expertise (fix the problem), develop a methodology to deal with such problems in the future, or learn how to think more productively and solve different types of problem, we hope that this book captures our experience, and helps you to become a better leader.

Acknowledgements

This book would not have emerged without the unstinting support of the many colleagues, friends and families who have contributed ideas, enthusiasm, encouragement, and a place for us to work, in particular:

Members of the Worshipful Company of Management Consultants

Patrick Chapman

Dennis Ciborowski

Elizabeth Consalvi

Ron Cruickshank

Denise Fellows

David Johnson

Calvert Markham

John Watson

Adrian Williams

Organisations

Cass Business School

RedQuadrant

The Haberdashers' Company

Business Colleagues

Nigel Bromley

Steve Hart

Greg Hoile

Graphic Designer – Natasa Sears

Cartoonist – T. Mclellan

*"Judge a man
by his questions,
not by his answers."*

Voltaire

Introduction

"Who wouldn't want a wireless security system".

"*If I had an hour to solve a problem I'd spend 55 minutes thinking about the problem and 5 minutes thinking about solutions.*" You've probably heard that attributed to Albert Einstein. He almost certainly never said it – but it underscores our point that problems are seldom what they seem.

To find better ideas for action, you need to understand the problem, go behind the surface level, find deeper causes, and think better. You need better questions.

At first glance, the questions in this book may not seem directly related to the situations listed. But think again! Consider why we suggest you ask yourself those questions. How might the questions help you better understand your situation?

How might the questions help you look at your problems with fresh eyes, as an outsider? How might the questions help you to dig deeper? How might you see things differently?

Successful and experienced leaders know that however a situation presents itself, there are likely to be hidden problems behind it. What better way to uncover these hidden depths than by asking questions that take you beyond the obvious?

This book isn't intended to be the advice a consultant, lawyer or mentor might offer at a moment of crisis, nor is it intended to be directive. Indeed, if you are reaching for this book in an urgent crisis, there are probably one or two other questions you might ask yourself!

This book does not contain the obvious questions and solutions you need in any situation. Our intention is to suggest some incisive questions that will lead you to find your own better answers to situations you face in business. The questions are generative so as to encourage divergent and creative critical thinking.

Though there can never be one right answer, there are right questions – which will help you find good answers.

How can I use this book?

Dip into it when you are stuck with a problem or need to resolve a situation, initiate a dialogue with others, stimulate ideas or find a route to an answer. Open it at random, browse through the questions – where do they lead you?

You could more logically start by identifying the situation you find yourself in. Is it something external, over which you have no control? Is it internal, something arising from inside? Does it involve a team of people? Or is it something personal? The book at a glance diagrams (pages 27-30) will help you find either your exact situation or something that approximates to it and from which you can work.

"Oh, well if you wanted to get here, I definitely wouldn't have started from there."

Having found your situation, try the suggested questions. Are there further questions those questions suggest?

Your answers to these questions should lead to action. If so, you now know how to use the book, the purpose of which is to influence people like yourself into more successful management!

Let's suppose you have just lost a major order that both you and your boss were certain you would win. You could ask your client why you were not chosen. You would then probably try and construct a cause and effect diagram to examine what led to the failure to secure the order. However, the diagram can only contain things you already know, it cannot give a new perspective on the problem. That is precisely where the questions in this book will help.

So, you reach for the book and begin by looking for an externally caused situation similar to the one you find yourself in. Situation 14, "I have just lost a major order" seems to be the one, but you may be attracted to other situations, such as situation 12 "A competitor arrives out of the blue", if the order was snatched by a competitor you did not see coming.

The situations, questions and sentences that surprise you, that you find interesting or that challenge you, will depend on your unique circumstances. You will find a selection of situations, questions and reasons for asking yourself the question. You will know which are right for you and your team.

Situation 14 suggests questions 9, 15, 30, 45, 92 or 98. Looking through these questions, certain sentences challenge you and your team. These may be question 9. "How adaptable is my organisation?"

At first glance, it may appear not to have anything to do with losing a major order; on the other hand, you may have a sneaky feeling that you are attached to your old and comfortable way of structuring the deal while your clients have moved on. What action does the question suggest to take? Only you will know.

From question 15. "What is the unique competence of my organization?" Am I using it to our best advantage? Has it changed? Only you will know what action to take.

Situation 12 suggests you ask yourself questions 9, 31, 38, 75, 81 or 94. Looking through the book, you see that question 81 looks interesting and you ask yourself, "What attracts customers and employees to my organisation?" You also notice that question 81 suggests you consider questions 15, 26 and 98. You see that question 26 looks interesting and so you ask yourself, "What astonishes me most about my organisation?" This may prompt you to view your issue from a different perspective and lead you to take an alternative action.

This simple example, which leads to you considering questions 9, 15 and 98 in the book, provides you with new insights into the situation, illustrates how the questions you ask yourself will invariably determine how you feel about a situation, and what you will do about it.

In summary, this book does not contain the obvious questions and solutions you need in any situation. It is a book of questions that will help you to develop a framework to focus on the real problems which lie behind any situation and from which you will find better answers.

Use this book as a workbook

As you ask yourself the questions in this book, you may find you want to jot down what comes up for you before you forget it. We have left plenty of white spaces in the book for you to do just that.

Questions you should ask yourself in any situation

We found that some questions are relevant to almost all situations.

To avoid repetition, they are listed below and excluded from the questions you will find under each situation.

2.   How do I measure success?

6.   What is the most searching question I could ask now?

19.   How would my people know I love them?

23.   Do I need more external advice?

24.   Could I use a mentor or coach ?

63.   What is my ideal outcome?

The book at a glance

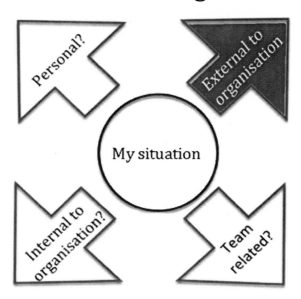

The numbers in bold refer to the questions you should consider asking yourself when faced with that situation.

Externally caused situations

1. My first hundred days. **10, 11,20, 70, 72, 95,**
2. I am going to a meeting with my most powerful shareholders. **5, 11, 47, 58, 59, 79**
3. I've received a takeover bid. **8, 13, 20, 31, 53, 96**
4. An external party raises doubts about the ability of a key member of my team. **16, 21, 36, 43, 60, 62**
5. I find myself in a completely new situation. **20, 52, 58, 64, 69, 87**
6. I find the same situation repeating itself. **9, 22, 52, 56, 67, 76**
7. A crisis arises which could destroy my team. **9, 11. 16. 54, 94**
8. An exciting acquisition target has emerged. **8, 55, 74, 79, 81**
9. I've just been contacted about a story in the media. **21, 26, 29, 30, 61, 81**
10. I need to build on my success. **47, 53, 55, 58, 86, 87**
11. Regulation is becoming more intrusive in my sector. **46, 49, 55, 74**
12. A competitor arrives out of the blue. **9, 31, 38, 75, 81, 94**

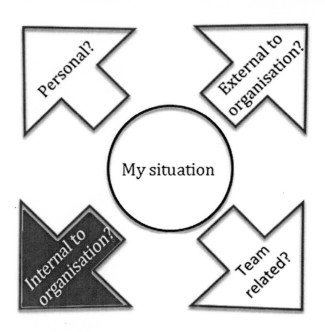

Situations internal to organisation

13. Our new product is such a success that traditional business is suffering. **8, 9, 22, 47, 52, 79**

14. I've just lost a major order. **9, 15, 30, 45, 92, 98**

15. I find a significant bad debt. **11, 17, 18, 56, 61, 65**

16. I have to issue a profit warning. **4, 9, 11, 17, 31, 47**

17. I need to raise finance. **8, 11, 15, 18, 30, 74**

18. I keep hitting barriers every time I grow. **8, 35, 55, 58, 86**

19. My product or service is out of date. **9, 15, 38, 55, 74, 98**

20. Too many opportunities keep emerging for my team to handle them. **8, 10, 52, 60, 71, 86**

21. I doubt that my advisers are truly independent. **21, 54, 61, 66, 77, 82**

22. I believe the values of my organisation are under threat. **1, 7, 30, 37, 90, 92**

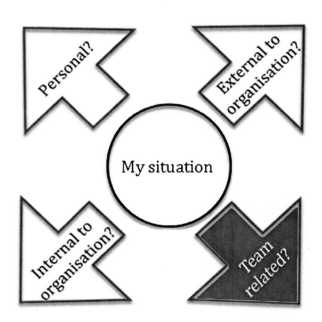

Team related situations

23. I am taking over a team and it has the wrong composition. **21, 58, 60, 66, 93, 81**
24. Morale among my team is very low. **16, 52, 71, 72, 83, 99**
25. I and my team find blockages at every turn. **9, 33, 62, 65, 71, 86**
26. I need to recruit a new team member. **8, 60, 61, 66, 74, 81**
27. My team keeps bringing me problems not solutions. **43, 60, 64, 67, 69, 72**
28. I seem to be the only one worried about a particular issue. **5, 46, 48, 86, 87**
29. I suspect that two of my team members are in a relationship. **1, 4, 7, 16, 21**
30. Someone has accused a team member of fraud. **7, 16, 21, 37, 71, 90**
31. There is a personal clash between two members of my team. **7, 88, 60, 61**
32. Differences in culture and/or values within my team cause problems. **7, 16, 43, 90, 92**
33. My team never gets to the long-term strategy because it is always dealing with the short term. **13, 48, 52, 55, 71**
34. My team leader has become wildly erratic. **7, 16, 60, 61, 88**
35. My team are all 'Yes men'. **21, 36, 60, 88**
36. There are a lot of threats and opportunities; my team needs to prioritise. **8, 15, 34, 47, 81**

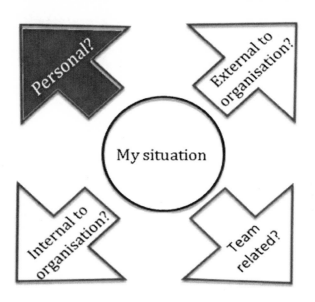

Personal situations

37. I doubt my competence in this situation. **20, 56, 59, 87**

38. I've been given six months to turn around the organisation. **8, 15, 31, 34, 52, 86**

39. I feel under considerable stress at work. **35, 52, 78, 80, 84, 91**

40. I think my boss is going to fire me. **64, 65, 82, 87**

41. My partner demands that I choose between them and my work. **73, 77, 82, 91, 97**

42. I have to take three months off. **14, 40, 51, 54, 87**

43. A key member has suddenly left. **3, 61, 66, 70, 72, 81**

44. I need a new challenge. **2, 53, 58, 76**

45. I have no one to talk to who will understand about my problems. **24, 65, 67, 77**

46. I need to find my successor. **3, 5, 11, 66**

47. I want to retire. **20, 39, 53**

Part One

SITUATIONS

SITUATIONS

These represent occasions when you might find yourself in need of new ideas or an external stimulus, e.g. to break a deadlock. They will be your own ideas that come, not from an external source but from asking yourself a few incisive questions.

External

Situations over which you have no control (1–12)

Internal

Situations that are internal to the organisation and over which you may have control (13–22)

Team

Situations relating to your team (23–36)

Personal

Situations that only you control (37–47)

EXTERNALLY CAUSED SITUATIONS

Situation 1.
My first hundred days

"Welcome to your first swimming lesson."

Day two. The excitement has passed and everyone is looking at her for solutions. She hopes she looks more confident than she feels as she is relying on them for the facts. But how will she know what the truth is?

She questions how she will meet the chair's brief, the shareholders' dreams, the analysts' crude focus on numbers, the board's wish to continue as they were yet to achieve more, the staff's wish for both leadership and approval, the customers' ever-changing must-haves, and how to reconcile all those with granny's enjoinder to stand out, blend in, and be loved by all. She wonders...

The tenure of leadership positions is shortening and will soon become less than the time it will take her to get her feet under the desk, so she must start as she means to go on.

Consider questions

10. What proportion of my staff can explain our business model?

11. Who are my five key stakeholders?

20. What would I like my legacy to be?

50. I am now the chief executive of my organisation; what two things will I do immediately?

70. Why should my people be committed to my organisation?

95. What is my predecessor's legacy?

Situation 2.
I am going to a meeting with my most powerful shareholders

Example 1

The executive board, backed by the full board, have agreed a high-risk diversification strategy. They are about to enter a financing agreement led by their bank. Their biggest shareholders are the family of the founder, who is now dead. The board does not want them to sell any shares.

So, how do the directors manage the meeting with them? They could shower them with flattery, take them to a very expensive restaurant, and impress them with brochures and photographs, with memories – and continuing appreciation – of the founder. All this to divert attention from the new strategy and secure their proxy votes for the next Annual General Meeting.

In the subsequent collapse of the diversification venture and near wipeout of the value of the shares, many people lose their jobs but the directors hang on to theirs. Well, the family are rich enough to survive – if not happily, then at least comfortably.

Example 2

They are a clever bunch of directors running a major not-for-profit organisation. How do they earn more? Ah! A plausible takeover target is identified. They meet their most powerful shareholders so that the votes at the Annual General Meeting are happily a foregone conclusion in favour of the takeover. With greatly increased turnover, their board salaries are doubled.

After a few years, it becomes obvious to all that the large subsidiary should be divested, so it is returned to the private sector. Some directors choose to leave with it, on even better terms. Everyone says that this is a perfect example of private aspirations leading to satisfactory outcomes for all.

Consider questions

1. Are my values aligned with those practised in my organisation?

5. What do I see over the horizon that others have not seen?

11. Who are my five key stakeholders?

47. Looking back from three years into the future, what three things did we do to achieve the success we had planned?

Situation 3.
I've received a takeover bid

The young, brash Texan chief executive of a small but ambitious software company had made a couple of million from selling his first internet business. He was certain that his entrepreneurial energies and unique technical insights would lead to a second and much greater business. He developed a business plan and selected a number of highly competent individuals who were ready to work with him on the basis of shared sweat equity.

A number of high-profile clients were approached and showed interest in what was being proposed. However, the cash flow aspects of the business plan were based on assumptions more likely to be valid in the US than the UK, and after a while it became clear that a significant injection of outside capital was going to be needed if the team and the promised offerings were to make it to market.

The burn rate eventually started to undermine confidence in the company's ability to achieve take off and an apparently friendly venture capitalist – who had been hovering in the wings – was asked to join the board. He immediately made a persuasive offer to the owner of the intellectual property in exchange for control.

The board reacted emotionally, deciding that it was not prepared to grant this carpetbagger his request so he disappeared – leaving the business in a state of disarray. Several board members subsequently resigned and the entrepreneur was left with lessons to ponder.

Consider questions

8. What are the current constraints on growth?

13. Why does my organisation need a goal other than survival?

20. What would I like my legacy to be?

31. What would the world be like without my organisation?

53. What is my unfulfilled dream?

96. What would my greatest competitor say about me?

"There is as much risk in doing nothing as in doing something."

Trammell Crow

Situation 4.
An external party raises doubts about the ability of a key member of my team

A mobile technology start-up was established in the UK by a South African holding company. The senior management team had initially all been South African; over time, as the business developed successfully, many of them left. One remaining member became increasingly disruptive and his performance dropped off, to the point that the owner raised doubts about his motivation and ability.

The senior management team tried, for a year, to help him overcome his difficulties through performance management, team-building events, coaching and mentoring. Eventually though, both the team and the manager realised that the solution was out of their hands and that the root cause of the problem was that the manager was missing his girlfriend, who had remained in South Africa.

The solution was for him to leave the UK and to return to South Africa. Dealing constructively with a disruptive team member was an important team-building exercise, though it might initially have seemed appropriate to have fired him for poor performance as soon as the owner complained.

Consider questions

16. How do I ensure the welfare of my team?

21. How do I know I am being told the truth?

36. What do I do to demonstrate that I take feedback seriously?

43. How much time do I allow my people for training and personal development?

60. What do I want from my team?

62. Who hasn't been heard on this issue?

"So before we discuss next weeks fraud investigation, the currently outstanding lawsuits filed against us, and that unfortunate fire in the canteen, I'd like to begin todays meeting with a little joke."

Situation 5.
I find myself in a completely new situation

"Vision without action is merely a dream.
Action without vision just passed the time.
Vision with action can change the world."

Joel Barker

Consider questions

20   What would I like my legacy to be?

38   How does innovation happen in my organisation?

52   How do I set, use and communicate priorities?

56. How do I learn?

64   What is expected of me around here?

69   What perceptions that others have of me would I like to correct?

Situation 6.
I find the same situation repeating itself

*"In times of rapid change,
experience could be your own worst enemy."*

J Paul Getty

*"Even if you're on the right track,
you'll get run over if you just sit there."*

Will Rogers

Consider questions

22.   Which top three adjectives would I use to describe success and failure in my organisation?

42.   What would cause me to consider leaving my job or changing careers?

56.   How do I learn?

67.   Which unwritten rules are helping or hurting me?

76.   What no longer works for me?

85.   How much time do I spend working on my business and how much working in it?

Situation 7.
A crisis arises which could destroy my team

"The things we fear most in organisations –
fluctuations, disturbances, imbalances –
are the primary sources of creativity."

Margaret J Wheatley

"People don't care how much you know
until they know how much you care."

Theodore Roosevelt

Consider questions

9.   How adaptable is my organisation?

11. Who are my five key stakeholders?

16. How do I ensure the welfare of my team?

54   What's my worst nightmare?

94   Who do I consult before taking difficult decisions?

Situation 8.
An exciting acquisition target has emerged

"Never have a strategic partner
with values different from yours."

Jerry Goldress

Iain's bankers telephoned him with the news that a rival with a recently reported difficulty was for sale and that the industry leader had been seen lunching with the rival's chief executive. Clearly, time was of the essence.

At the hastily convened board meeting, the non-executives were keen to bid, largely to prevent market share going to the rival. Others were less enthusiastic about the merger.

The chair and Iain worked together to analyse the situation and were not sanguine about the chances of the acquisition meeting the board's strategic goals, doubting that the supposed strategic synergy would be realised.

Iain managed to persuade the board not to be seduced by this opportunity; he stressed that the acquisition would be a white elephant. Two years later, the eventual acquirer's business folded, pulled down by its acquisition.

Consider questions

8. What are the current constraints on growth?

25. Which organisation do I most admire?

55. How do I survive and flourish by changing faster than my environment?

74. What are the likely future changes in my business landscape?

79. If I could invest £100K to promote competitiveness, what would I spend it on?

81. What attracts customers and employees to my organisation?

Situation 9.
I've just been contacted about a story in the media

Jean, the company secretary, was working late in the office on a Friday evening. Answering the telephone, she heard, "Oh, I am so glad I caught you, Mrs Campbell. Thank you for answering my call. I am Tony Brookes from the technical section of *Finance News*. We heard that your company, NewTech plc, is being approached by GiantTech. Please would you confirm this?"

Well, NewTech did not employ a PR manager. The managing director did have a tame PR consultant – who had addressed the board twice. Fortunately, Jean had not been distracted during these presentations so she remembered what he had said about the right way to respond to such an approach, as well as the desired outcomes. Although she knew of *Finance News*, she had no knowledge of Tony Brookes.

"Well, Mr Brookes, I am busy, but it is good to hear of your interest in NewTech. I must be brief, but will try and help you. Since we launched TechFive at the industry fair in March, there has indeed been a lot of interest in our technology. As you may know, we again increased our turnover by 50% in the year to 31 March. I am therefore not surprised to hear about your rumour. Incidentally, from whom did you hear this story? It is always worth knowing where we are being talked about."

(Long pause)

"Mr Brookes, thank you for your interest, I must now finish what I was doing. If you would like us to go through any details in your piece before the deadline, then we could help by having it checked for accuracy and get straight back to you at *Finance News*. Goodbye."

Consider questions

21. How do I know I am being told the truth?

26. What astonishes me most about my organisation?

29. I am in a coffee shop and start talking to a stranger. I am asked what my organisation does. Can I answer this in 30 seconds such that the stranger says 'tell me more'?

30. Why am I proud of the organisation for which I work?

61. Is there something not being said?

81. What attracts customers and employees to my organisation?

"Most people treat the news media like the exercise bike they have in their basement. They're glad it's there but they never use it."

Drew Curtis

Situation 10.
I need to build on my success

As IT director of a large financial institution, Sebastian convinced the board that they needed to integrate their network of branches with the head office in order to both reduce clerical labour costs and increase their levels of customer service. After a prolonged evaluation of the options available, they selected the latest in a series of successful retail terminal products that appeared well-integrated into the existing infrastructure and supplier relationships.

Within a short period of time, the team that had made the sale moved on and a new grouping was introduced. The technical challenges that began to emerge created considerable uncertainty for the customer and real concern for the supplier that a critical relationship was in jeopardy.

An energetic and technically competent relationship manager was brought in to lead the supplier's team. She quickly re-established excellent working relationships at all levels by combining transparency of the problems the supplier was facing with positive leadership of the combined implementation team. Eventually, this highly successful joint project became a reference site and all members of the team were recognised and promoted.

Consider questions

47. Looking back from three years into the future, what three things did we do to achieve the success we had planned?

53. What is my unfulfilled dream?

55. How do I survive and flourish by changing faster than my environment?

58. If I were guaranteed success, what would I attempt?

86. What's getting in the way of me getting things done and reaching my and the organisation's potential?

87. What is my unique contribution?

"Would you like me to give you a formula for success?
It's quite simple, really.
Double your rate of failure!"

Thomas J. Watson

"These new financial regulations have been great practise at finding new ways around financial regulations."

Situation 11.
Regulation is becoming more intrusive in my sector

Universities in the UK have come under increasing financial pressure as the Government reduces grants for further education. Those universities with a strong global educational reputation seek to attract foreign students to bolster their income.

However, national concerns over immigration have brought a flood of regulations. These directives, from visa quotas to Tier 4 rating conditions and UK Border Agency (UKBA) Highly Trusted Status (HTS), have pushed up costs significantly. London Metropolitan University was almost forced to close when it lost its HTS because some of its overseas students did not respect UKBA reporting regulations.

Consider questions

46. To which uncertainty affecting my organisation would I most like the answer?

49. What one thing could the Government do that would help us to succeed?

55. How do I survive and flourish by changing faster than my environment?

74. What are the likely future changes in my business landscape?

Situation 12.
A competitor arrives out of the blue

In the UK, it was usual for people with mortgages to have two separate accounts with financial institutions: a current and/or savings account usually in the black, and a mortgage account, in the red until the mortgage is paid off. In the late 90s, Virgin, an outsider and consequently not considered to be a potential competitor, changed all that. Virgin teamed up with a bank to offer a single mortgage and current account, the Virgin One account.

This meant that all money in the previously non-interest bearing current account was now earning the same interest rate as that charged for the mortgage. Within a few years, all financial institutions changed the structure of their mortgage/current/savings account products.

Consider questions

9.   How adaptable is my organisation?

31.   What would the world be like without my organisation?

38.   How does innovation happen in my organisation?

75.   Is it time to change our winning strategy?

81.   What attracts customers and employees to my organisation?

94.   How can I measure the resilience of my organisation?

SITUATIONS INTERNAL TO THE ORGANISATION

Situation 13.
Our new product is such a success that traditional business is suffering

Example 1

Brewers used to have tied pubs through which there was a guaranteed outlet for their own brewed beers. As a result of threats from the competition, authorities and the success of Free Houses that sold a variety of beers, the brewers gradually relinquished the 'tie' on their pubs.

Many of these pubs became successful and the brewers realised that they now had a significant investment in their outlets. Over time, many brewers moved completely out of brewing (their traditional business that was declining) and concentrated on managing profitable pubs; in many cases, some even moved into areas such as hotels, fast food, coffee shops, etc.

Example 2

Many years ago, Midland Bank (now part of HSBC) had the largest branch network of any UK retail bank – and it promoted this fact. It also foresaw that technology might change the nature of banking. It sought a way of capitalising on the latter while retaining its branch network strength. The solution was to create First Direct (a telephone banking service) that was separately branded from Midland Bank. When First Direct significantly reduced the demand for Midland Bank branches, the network of Midland Bank branches was slashed.

Consider questions

8. What are the current constraints on growth?

9. How adaptable is my organisation?

22. Which top three adjectives would I use to describe success and failure in my organisation?

47. Looking back from three years into the future, what three things did we do to achieve the success we had planned?

52. How do I set, use and communicate priorities?

79. If I could invest £100K to promote competitiveness, what would I spend it on?

Situation 14.
I've just lost a major order

"Competitive advantage is an ability to learn faster than competitors."

Gary Hamel

*"There is only one boss. The customer.
And he can fire everybody in the company
from the chairman down,
simply by spending her own money somewhere else."*

Sam Walton

Consider questions

9.   How adaptable is my organisation?

15. What is the unique competence of my organisation?

30. Why am I proud of the organisation for which I work?

45. How should I target the 'right' customers, internal and external?

92. What aspects of the culture of my organisation attract customers?

98. How do I learn about my customers' needs?

Situation 15.
I've found a significant bad debt

"The minute you settle for less than you deserve, you get even less than you settled for."

Maureen Dowd

Consider questions

11. Who are my five key stakeholders?

17. How can I ensure that everyone understands the profit and loss statement?

18. What is the first thing I could do to improve cash flow?

56. How do I learn?

61. Is there something not being said?

65. If I fail to perform, where do I go for help?

Situation 16.
I have to issue a profit warning

"Where there is no vision, the people perish."

Proverbs 29:18

They have always prided themselves on their management information systems that deliver 'the full pack' five working days after the month end and in plenty of time for the non-executives to review before their board meeting on the third Thursday of the month. Their plans, forecasts and budgets are prepared in full consultation with the teams and refined in an iterative process over the last six months of each financial year.

The finance director has just alerted the chief executive to the significant deviation from plan that last month's (month 9) cumulative flash figures will reveal when they are released in two days' time. They will not be able to recoup the shortfall over the remaining three months of this year and so the chief executive will have to alert the chair and the board, and the senior team, some of whose partners had mentally spent their expected bonuses, and issue a profit warning to our bankers, brokers and the market. The headhunters, who have so far wooed the chief executive, will mark his card accordingly.

The panic and the sinking, sick feeling felt by the chief executive were somewhat relieved by a quick telephone conversation with his 'better half'. He worked with his colleagues to limit the immediate damage and make sure they learned from this episode. One lesson was to drive the business forward by looking through the windscreen rather than the rear-view mirror.

Consider questions

4.   What would I rather others did not know?

9.   How adaptable is my organisation?

11. Who are my five key stakeholders?

17. How can I ensure that everyone understands the profit and loss statement?

31. What would the world be like without my organisation?

47. Looking back from three years into the future, what three things did we do to achieve the success we had planned?

"If there were any other investors in town, I'd recommend you use them."

Situation 17.
I need to raise finance

They were boffins, with big reputations in their field. To fulfil their dream, they dreamt big. They formed a top level international team and threatened a country that if they did not back them with a massive grant, they would go elsewhere. They thought through their promotional process, using their few dollars for expensive process advice. The country representatives were convinced by their appeal. They also negotiated well, giving away on tactical issues but preserving their international strategy.

Once formed, they were technically highly successful but ran into political as well as commercial difficulties. They had not raised enough finance to focus on their breakthrough product, let alone to compete with their biggest competitors. One of these eventually bought them out, moving much of the creative work outside the country which had backed them.

Does every story have to have a clean resolution? No. Business life is often messy. Perhaps their strategy was too technical and lacked sufficient commercial ambition and process definition.

Consider questions

8.   What are the current constraints on growth?

11.   Who are my five key stakeholders?

15.   What is the unique competence of my organisation?

18.   What is the first thing I could do to improve cash flow?

30.   Why am I proud of the organisation for which I work?

74.   What are the likely future changes in my business landscape?

Situation 18.
I keep hitting barriers every time I grow

As the third largest supplier of IT services to global customers, IT Max found themselves in the position of having won business against the odds in a distant country. The managing director was invited to sponsor the implementation of the project that had previously been negotiated between the IT Max regional representative and the client.

He was faced with a dilemma after an internal audit revealed how far the project was from the team's core competence. Refusing to support the project would be a career limiting move. Agreeing to go ahead would take him and his team far from their comfort zone. In the end, he decided that he had little choice but to proceed. However, success was highly dependent on local cooperation which proved a major challenge. Year-end sales pressures forced the managing director to sign off the deal before the full requirement was understood.

Conflicts in divisional management objectives meant that the internal capabilities needed were not released. At the same time, the external competencies needed proved hard to obtain within the agreed budget.

The eventual size and complexity of the project was out of all proportion to the management structures and processes that had been adequate for previous well-understood projects. Reinventing them on the hoof was one step beyond what could be achieved. A post-implementation review gave them this choice: either to avoid similar step change opportunities, or to create a new approach to undertaking such high risk projects with their associated profitability.

Consider questions

8. What are the current constraints on growth?

35. When something goes wrong, how do I know if it's important?

55. How do I survive and flourish by changing faster than my environment?

58. If I were guaranteed success, what would I attempt?

86. What's getting in the way of me getting things done and reaching my and the organisation's potential?

Situation 19.
My product or service is out of date

The owner of an Irish funeral parlour realised that the demand for his services was much higher in winter than in summer – but it was not within his power to change this pattern of demand!

He took a long hard look at his assets – primarily a fleet of luxury black limousines, a hearse and a deep knowledge of Irish parishes. As an experiment, after a little market research, he decided to offer a service in the summer to Irish Americans visiting Ireland in search of their ancestral roots. He would meet them at the airport and transport them in his limousines to search various possible parish records.

The business flourished, though he still hasn't found an alternative use for the hearse!

Consider questions

9.   How adaptable is my organisation?

15.   What is the unique competence of my organisation?

38.   How does innovation happen in my organisation?

55.   How do I survive and flourish by changing faster than my environment?

74.   What are the likely future changes in my business landscape?

98.   How do I learn about my customers' needs?

Situation 20.
Too many opportunities keep emerging for my team to handle them

"Killing off a project is harder than starting one."

Simon Majaro

Thomas J. Watson, founder of IBM, once said, "Would you like me to give you a formula for success? It's quite simple, really. Double your rate of failure. You're thinking of failure as the enemy of success. But it isn't at all... You can be discouraged by failure – or you can learn from it. So go ahead and make mistakes. Make all you can. Because, remember that's where you'll find success."

Consider questions

8. What are the current constraints on growth?

10. What proportion of my staff can explain our business model?

52. How do I set, use and communicate priorities?

60. What do I want from my team?

71. What do I tolerate round here that gets in the way?

86. What's getting in the way of me getting things done and reaching my and the organisation's potential?

Situation 21.
I doubt that my advisers are truly independent

As a board member of an SME, Jim found the behaviour of one of the directors difficult to fathom. The company had been approached by a number of organisations interested in acquiring them following the shareholders' decision to sell. The most assiduous of these was a competitor that had put far too generous an offer on the table. Jim knew from experience that the sum would be gradually eroded as the due diligence progressed, so was unimpressed by their lack of professionalism.

The director in question, usually cautious, was uncharacteristically anxious to proceed with the competitor's offer and seemed to be on very familiar terms with the competitor's finance director. Jim suspected that they had made some sort of deal. This was never proved, but the competitor's finance director was fired shortly afterwards.

Consider questions

21. How do I know I am being told the truth?

54. What's my worst nightmare?

61. Is there something not being said?

66. How would I like to change the cast of players?

77. What do I really want from my relationships?

82. What am I pretending not to know or to see?

Situation 22.
I believe the values of my organisation are under threat

"Living values over-rules rules."

Anon

"The biggest mistake a manager can make is to back down on a matter of principle."

Clarence Francis

Consider questions

1. Are my values aligned with those practised in my organisation?

7. What do I do when the behaviour of others clashes with policies, procedures or culture?

30. Why am I proud of the organisation for which I work?

37. How do my actions support the culture of my organisation?

90. What do I do to embed our values and ethics?

92. What aspects of the culture of my organisation attract customers?

TEAM SITUATIONS

"I think we need an alternative but equally uninformed opinion."

"The first method for estimating the intelligence of a ruler is to look at the men he has around him."

Niccolò Machiavelli

Situation 23.
I am taking over a team
and suspect it has the wrong composition

"First they ignore you.
Then they laugh at you.
Then they fight you.
Then you win."

Mahatma Gandhi

Consider questions

21. How do I know I am being told the truth?

58. If I were guaranteed success, what would I attempt?

60. What do I want from my team?

66. How would I like to change the cast of players?

81. What attracts customers and employees to my organisation?

93. Who do I consult before taking difficult decisions?

Situation 24.
Morale among my team is very low

The team leader had screwed up. He was stuck with half his new team in a foreign airport with no scheduled connection to their destination. They had to see their client within 48 hours. To get to the client, they had to cross a war zone. Morale was at rock bottom.

During the subsequent, hair-raising, 24-hour journey, a transformation took place. Under stress, the team gelled; the new members at the destination were quickly absorbed. The client was impressed and the team never looked back. They had 'formed, stormed and normed' in one day. They developed and carried forward a level of communication, interdependency and trust, ideally suited to the job. On this most demanding assignment, they were exceptionally productive and achieved all key performance indicators.

Consider questions

16. How do I ensure the welfare of my team?

52. How do I set, use and communicate priorities?

71. What do I tolerate round here that gets in the way?

72. What do I do to encourage others to use their gifts?

83. What decision am I avoiding?

99. Do I ask my team how my actions make them feel?

Situation 25.
I and my team find blockages at every turn

A vertically integrated textile group based in Hong Kong comprised a large group of companies with complex cross-shareholdings and management structure. A consultant was employed to look at ways of improving management information flows.

She interviewed representatives of all functions at all levels. In each case, the interviewees justified what they were doing but implied that their colleagues were the problem, without being specific. It was only at a social event, talking to an intern, that one name kept cropping up in the conversation, that of a long-serving office manager at group headquarters. The consultant started investigating further and found that the office manager had put himself at the centre of an informal network that gave him status beyond his authority. In this way, he was able to influence and effectively block any initiatives that could change the status quo.

Consider questions

9. How adaptable is my organisation?

33. Who are the influencers in my organisation?

62. Who hasn't been heard on this issue?

65. If I fail to perform, where do I go for help?

71. What do I tolerate round here that gets in the way?

86. What's getting in the way of me getting things done and reaching my and the organisation's potential?

Situation 26.
I need to recruit a new team member

With Didier Drogba due to leave Chelsea Football Club in the summer of 2011, the team needed a top striker to replace him. Backed by their Russian oligarch owner, money was no object. In January 2011, for a £50 million transfer fee, Chelsea hired Fernando Torres from Liverpool. At his best, Torres was among the finest in the world. The goal that he scored and that won Euro 2008 for Spain was terrific. When Fernando Torres moved to Chelsea, this supremely talented footballer struggled to recapture his legendary form which had made him worth the figure paid for his services.

Successfully replacing a team member is not just about finding a brilliant individual. It's about ensuring that the new member fits with the existing team. "A star team is more effective than a team of stars."

Consider questions

8. What are the current constraints on growth?

61. Is there something not being said?

66. How would I like to change the cast of players?

74. What are the likely future changes in my business landscape?

81. What attracts customers and employees to my organisation?

89. How do I respond to diversity issues?

Situation 27.
My team keeps bringing me problems, not solutions

A manager operated an 'open-door policy', both physically and as part of his management style. Admirable as this might be, he was rarely left in peace by his team members who kept bringing him their problems. Moreover, he could usually find a solution – sometimes quite easily.

In an enlightened moment, he decided that he would only see a team member if a possible solution, however unrealistic, was also presented to him. The volume of people coming through his door significantly diminished – and his team members grew in their learning.

Consider questions

40. What would be the consequences if I took three months off?

43. How much time do I allow my people for training and personal development?

60. What do I want from my team?

67. Which unwritten rules are helping or hurting me?

69. What perceptions that others have of me would I like to correct?

72. What do I do to encourage others to use their gifts?

Situation 28.
I seem to be the only one worried about a particular issue

"Vision is the art of seeing things invisible."

Jonathan Swift

"A moment's insight is sometimes worth a life's experience."

Oliver Wendell Holmes

Consider questions

5.   What do I see over the horizon that others have not seen?

32.   If I were the sole owner of my organisation, what one thing would I change?

46.   To which uncertainty affecting my organisation would I most like the answer?

48.   Looking back from three years into the future, everything has gone terribly for our organisation. What did I fail to do?

86.   What's getting in the way of me getting things done and reaching my and the organisation's potential?

87.   What is my unique contribution?

Situation 29.
I suspect that two of my team members are in a relationship

While on an assignment in a manufacturing firm, a consultant had a conversation with a woman who had been promoted to being a supervisor the year before. She confided that she had faced unforeseen difficulty after her appointment as supervisor, because one of her team members was also her partner.

She had thought that he would be happy at her promotion, but from the moment she became a supervisor he became resentful. To deal with it, she sat down with her partner and explained that, while there had indeed been a significant change in their professional relationship, she still felt the same about their personal relationship and asked her partner to accept this. It wasn't easy, but through her openness and honesty, she was able to reconnect with her partner and they both came to see her promotion in a positive light.

Consider questions

1. Are my values aligned with those practised in my organisation?

4. What would I rather others did not know?

7. What do I do when the behaviour of others clashes with policies, procedures or culture?

16. How do I ensure the welfare of my team?

21. How do I know I am being told the truth?

"It's O.K. So long as it doesn't affect your work."

Situation 30.
Someone has accused a team member of fraud

"An objection is not a rejection;
it is simply a request for more information."

Bo Bennett

The quarterly board meeting had been probing but, as the team members departed rather earlier than was usual, there was a sense of 'a good job well done'. It also allowed the chair to catch a flight before the weekend rush. The executive directors returned to their offices to make the most of the unexpectedly available time.

However, at 17.50, John, the finance director, poked his head round the chief executive's door and asked if the chief executive could spare him a few minutes. He looked ashen-faced. As he was reaching for a chair, the chief executive wondered why problems tended to rear their heads late on a Friday afternoon.

John laid out his afternoon's findings with his customary impeccable logic and described how examining all the possible alternatives led to one inescapable conclusion – one of their fellow directors, aided by one of his team, had diverted substantial sums of money from the company to another enterprise of which they were shareholders. The adrenalin kicked in immediately and the urgent preparation of statements and initiation of legal processes was executed crisply and confidently.

By Sunday evening, there was time for reflection and questioning. How could such trusted colleagues, even friends, with whom he had socialised, cheat like this? The chief executive had chosen the whole team and was proud to have each one on board. Indeed, was he prejudging the position? After all, those accused had not yet been approached.

NAAAF, the chief executive thought: Never Assume, Always Ask First!

Consider questions

7. What do I do when the behaviour of others clashes with policies, procedures or culture?

16. How do I ensure the welfare of my team?

21. How do I know I am being told the truth?

37. How do my actions support the culture of my organisation?

71. What do I tolerate round here that gets in the way?

90. What do I do to embed our values and ethics?

Situation 31.
There is a personal clash between two members of my team.

The clash was between two older team members of the team and a third younger member. The older two had worked together for several years in the industry. The third member was new to the industry and to the team. He was appointed team leader on the basis that he would implement the recommendations. All three seemed to be working together successfully in a remote location and to a demanding schedule. Towards the end, the third member took a short pre-arranged holiday.

The established two then used their network to oust the younger member. In the short term, this led to a happier team, but in the longer term it damaged the company's interests as the implementation had to be handed over to a third party.

Consider questions

7. What do I do when the behaviour of others clashes with policies, procedures or culture?

60. What do I want from my team?

61. Is there something not being said?

88. How do I encourage constructive dissent in my organisation?

"Of course, this is an open forum. I'd love to hear your thoughts, even though I've already decided _exactly_ what I'm going to do".

Situation 32.
Differences in culture and/or values within my team cause problems

Running a multinational team can be tricky. There were sensitive Chinese clients and very direct American ex-forces personnel engaged in testing the security of a product. The Chinese found the Americans arrogant and deliberately offensive, while the Americans found the Chinese unable to understand how important it was to get to the bottom of potentially serious flaws that had been allowed to accumulate.

This led to an impasse, which was resolved by the Australians and the British, whose greater multicultural exposure was accepted by all parties. Their diplomacy established the trust that enabled them to resolve the issue.

Consider questions

7. What do I do when the behaviour of others clashes with policies, procedures or culture?

16. How do I ensure the welfare of my team?

43. How much time do I allow my people for training and personal development?

89. How do I respond to diversity issues?

90. What do I do to embed our values and ethics?

92. What aspects of the culture of my organisation attract customers?

Situation 33.
My team never gets to the long-term strategy because it is always dealing with the short-term

The military is notorious for inculcating a culture of 'you must act'. "What is your plan?", "What are you going to do?" are constant questions asked of junior leaders. A response of "I'm going to do nothing," or "I'm going to wait and see," is not likely to lead to promotion.

In reality, the 'do nothing' option can be the best one, or certainly the 'least worst' one, and should never be discounted too early in a planning process. A positive decision to do nothing, as opposed to indecision that results in a 'do nothing option' by default, can be a brave and sensible course of action. It also frees up time to work on the long-term strategy.

Consider questions

13. Why does my organisation need a goal other than survival?

48. Looking back from three years into the future, everything has gone terribly for our organisation. What did I fail to do?

52. How do I set, use and communicate priorities?

55. How do I survive and flourish by changing faster than my environment?

71. What do I tolerate round here that gets in the way?

Situation 34.
My team leader has become wildly erratic

Erraticness can be the result of a variety of challenges. A chief executive was addressing some six hundred members of senior management at a conference about his proposed shift in the organisation's culture. At one point in his presentation, he said, "I'll kill the next person who says that I operate a fear culture!"

Consider questions

7. What do I do when the behaviour of others clashes with policies, procedures or culture?

16. How do I ensure the welfare of my team?

60. What do I want from my team?

61. Is there something not being said?

88. How do I encourage constructive dissent in my organisation?

Situation 35.
My team are all 'yes men'

The shareholders loved our chief executive. He was charming, spoke passionately about the company, and was an engaging storyteller. He had started as a salesman and worked his way up through the ranks. His presentations were excellent, but there was something missing: they were too perfect. Everything he wanted to cover was very neatly wrapped up and tied in a bow. How could anyone spoil such a beautiful parcel by tearing away the paper?

Listening was the only option; the presentation could not be spoilt by questions. Although not everyone was taken by the neatness of the presentation and some did ask questions, the chief executive soon put a halt to that by marginalising the curious. Consequently, he now rarely needs to deal with conflict in his management meetings. As people do not tell him what he does not want to hear, he does not know what is really going on. Occasionally he wonders why he cannot change the downward trajectory of the company.

Consider questions

21. How do I know I am being told the truth?

36. What do I do to demonstrate that I take feedback seriously?

40. What would be the consequences if I took 3 months off?

60. What do I want from my team?

68. How do other people's perceptions of my power in the organisation affect the things I do?

88. How do I encourage constructive dissent in my organisation?

Situation 36.
There are a lot of threats and opportunities; my team needs to prioritise

"The only difference between stumbling blocks and stepping stones is the way that we use them."

Anon

Consider questions

8. What are the current constraints on growth?

15. What is the unique competence of my organisation?

34. Imagine that consultants have fairy dust that they can sprinkle over your organisation to change it in any way you want. What would you like it to do for yours?

47. Looking back from three years into the future, what three things did we do to achieve the success we had planned?

81. What attracts customers and employees to my organisation?

PERSONAL SITUATIONS

Situation 37.
I doubt my competence in this situation

*"Your attitude, not your aptitude,
will determine your altitude."*

Zig Ziglar

Consider questions

20. What would I like my legacy to be?

42. What would cause me to consider leaving my job or changing careers?

56. How do I learn?

59. How am I doing and how do I know?

87. What is my unique contribution?

Situation 38.
I've been given six months to turn around the organisation

The company had been the major contributor to group profits. No longer: the figures had turned unexpectedly red. The group bottom line was suffering.

The new group managing director had six months to effect a turnaround. She had not yet established her authority in this important subsidiary. Investigations would be time-consuming but the status quo could not continue. Under a plausible cover story concerning facilities, she sent a bright young consultant to investigate.

He found that a core cross-department procurement process was dysfunctional. They initiated a formal review of core processes and appointed a new divisional chief executive who had demonstrated experience of managing processes. This improvement initiative led to a return to profits within six months. Happier times.

Consider questions

8. What are the current constraints on growth?

15. What is the unique competence of my organisation?

31. What would the world be like without my organisation?

34. Imagine that consultants have fairy dust that they can sprinkle over your organisation to change it in any way you want. What would you like it to do for yours?

52. How do I set, use and communicate priorities?

86. What's getting in the way of me getting things done and reaching my and the organisation's potential?

"Some of our new staff are struggling with their work/home balance."

Situation 39.
I feel under considerable stress at work

There was a major European product launch coming up. Dates and locations had been agreed and the divisional director had lined up the senior European executives to provide a high-profile launch.

He was to host the event as well as give the keynote speech and act as master of ceremonies. The information packages were being assembled without the pricing information, which would be added by the back office team on the day. However, when the day arrived, there was no back office team due to a sudden onset of sickness.

To maintain the appearance of control and complete confidence until the end of the event, the divisional director had to co-opt others who were fully occupied and who had no knowledge of the missing information. They carried it off perfectly, but felt grey and drawn for weeks afterwards.

And this is only one example of what happens all too frequently.

Consider questions

27.   Do I take all my annual leave?

35.   When something goes wrong, how do I know if it's important?

78.   How much longer before I live the life I want to but haven't because of all the things I've had to do?

80.   What are my frustrations and disappointments?

84.   What's working well for me at the moment?

91.   How often do I say 'No' and how do I say it?

Situation 40.
I think my boss is going to fire me

Are these telltale signs? Duncan is being excluded from important emails and notices of meetings, and being blamed for things that aren't his fault. How does he read these signs? Is he being paranoid? Does he have enemies? Or is he just incompetent?

Consider questions

28. When on holiday, how often do I access my emails?

64. What is expected of me around here?

65. If I fail to perform, where do I go for help?

82. What am I pretending not to know or to see?

87. What is my unique contribution?

Situation 41.
My partner demands that I choose between them and my work

The chief executive of a large organisation had become increasingly disenchanted with his work and was also under pressure to spend more time with his family – both situations were unsatisfactory. After a long discussion with his wife, he quit his job. All went well for a couple of years until his wife complained that they could no longer afford the life to which they had become accustomed. A few years later, they were divorced. Would it have been better if the issue had been properly discussed right at the start?

Consider questions

41. Am I a workaholic or do I just love my job?

73. Are my priorities consistent with my purpose in life?

77. What do I really want from my relationships?

82. What am I pretending not to know or to see?

91. How often do I say 'No' and how do I say it?

97. How do I balance 'work' and 'life'?

"Welcome to WORKAHOLICS ANONYMOUS."

Situation 42.
I have to take three months off

Poor Jonathan Bloomer, Prudential's former chief executive, found himself on the receiving end of criticism in spring 2001, when he took off on holiday in the Caribbean. He thought he and his family deserved a break – a £14 billion takeover of American General had been agreed. Alas, while he was on the beach, a US rival, AIG, slapped in a higher offer. Bloomer hopped on the first plane home but not in time to stop the critics muttering that he should not have left his post until his own deal had been signed off.

In fact, even if he had remained tied to his desk, he would not have been able to prevent AIG making a more attractive offer for American General. He might, however, have been able to persuade investors to warm to his bid and thereby lift Prudential's share price and the value of its offer. Bloomer had planned to do the rounds of the investors once he returned, suntanned, from Barbados, but by then it was too late. He now regrets the loss of American General, but not the holiday, and he reasons that no amount of effort would have enabled him to defeat AIG.

Consider questions

14. Who is really my boss?

40. What would be the consequences if I took three months off?

51. How would I brief a person who is replacing me for a few months about this 'issue'?

54. What's my worst nightmare?

87. What is my unique contribution?

Situation 43.
A key member has suddenly left

He was the 'hero' – the techie, the geek – who loved solving problems that baffled everyone else. He never complained when called at an improbable hour and asked to travel halfway round the world to sort out a client's quality problem. He was known throughout the organisation for his technical expertise, and then... he was asked to share it, to teach others, to form a team of experts. The only surprise was that it took so many years for the company to become aware of the cost of the 'hero'. The clients were happy and gave excellent feedback, but he did not share what he had learned with his colleagues. The solutions to recurring errors were not recorded as a matter of course. However, the new approach, which recognised all this and did not put 'heroes' on a pedestal caused him to leave – before training his successors.

Consider questions

3. Do I understand why the top people are in their positions?

61. Is there something not being said?

66. How would I like to change the cast of players?

70. Why should my people be committed to my organisation?

72. What do I do to encourage others to use their gifts?

81. What attracts customers and employees to my organisation?

Situation 44.
I need a new challenge

*"To grow, you must be willing
to let your present and future
be totally unlike your past.
Your history is not your destiny."*

Alan Cohen

The young founder/owner of a fast-growing group had doubled his turnover every year in each of the past four years by seizing every opportunity and delegating meaningfully to the members of his bright and dedicated team.

During a coaching session, he sounded jaded and admitted that the thought of doing the same every year for the next thirty-five years did not appeal to him. The growth of the business was no longer a challenge. Ranging over life in general, he decided that major single-handed yachting events would provide the stimulation he was seeking. He restructured all operations and with the deadline for submission of the application forms for one race only nine months ahead, he challenged his team to accept further responsibility for running 'their' units within eight months.

After winning the first race, he celebrated with the whole team and decided that in the future he would have his cake and eat it. By remaining hands-off in the business, he elevated his role to that of chair – with new and different challenges – and did the deals, entrusting others to make them work. The rate of growth increased still further.

He also had more time for sailing and buying larger boats for even more difficult races.

Consider questions

25. Which organisation do I most admire?

42. What would cause me to consider leaving my job or changing careers?

53. What is my unfulfilled dream?

58. If I were guaranteed success, what would I attempt?

76. What no longer works for me?

"Apparently I've gone viral!? Do I need an ambulance?"

Situation 45.
I have no one to talk to who will understand about my problems

Being an introvert, Paul may recognise the need to share problems with his colleagues. However, this is easier with technical and formal issues than with many of the problems that concern relationships and confidential information. Attending a lecture on networks by an engineering professor, Paul was struck by her use of the phrase 'the power of weak links'. This made him aware that he had been too limiting in considering with whom he could share his problems.

So he searched his own strong and weaker networks for anyone in a position to share his confidential information and problems. A couple of names emerged, and contact with them led to one agreeing to engage with him informally and to another becoming his mentor.

Mentoring has helped Paul to acknowledge his problems and understand their underlying causes. His mentor also ensures that he is fully committed to their resolution or acceptance. He feel more empowered. The mentor arrangement is coming to a natural end. Some problems have gone away, proving unreal or insignificant. Others have been recognised and are being addressed for the first time.

Consider questions

44. How do I encourage value from our non-executives?

65. If I fail to perform, where do I go for help?

67. Which unwritten rules are helping or hurting me?

77. What do I really want from my relationships?

"We can't even find anyone qualified enough to replace him."

Situation 46.
I need to find my successor

"When the path is clear,
anyone can be the leader.
In the middle of ambiguity,
leadership is visible.
The person who paints
the clearest picture of reality
will emerge as the leader."

Tom Foster

Consider questions

3. Do I understand why the top people are in their positions?

5. What do I see over the horizon that others have not seen?

11. Who are my five key stakeholders?

12. Is the spread of length of service of my senior team appropriate?

32. If I were the sole owner of my organisation what one thing would I change?

66. How would I like to change the cast of players?

Situation 47.
I want to retire

The chair of a management consulting firm wanted to retire but was worried about how to pass the responsibility over to his managing partners. He decided to tell them that he had determined a new strategy for the firm but wanted the managing partners to have six weeks to develop their own plan before he implemented his.

After six weeks, a comprehensive plan was ready and was accepted by the chair. He never disclosed his plan and was able to retire three months later safe in the knowledge that the managing partners had taken over and the future of the firm was assured.

Consider questions

20.   What would I like my legacy to be?

39.   What are the first three things I would suggest my successor reviews?

53.   What is my unfulfilled dream?

Part Two

QUESTIONS

QUESTIONS

1. Are my values aligned with those practised in my organisation?

Why ask myself this question?

Because my work is an expression of myself; any misalignment means that:

I cannot contribute my best,

I live with contradictions,

Communication with team members is impaired.

Consequently, I and my organisation both suffer loss of potential.

To place myself where I can best contribute, I might need to change myself or influence my organisation's or my team's values. It may even mean my moving to a more compatible organisation.

Consider also questions: 30, 37, 90

What insights might I expect to gain?

Being able to distinguish between my organisation's espoused and its practised values.

A better understanding of how important my values are to me.

Enable me to question my own values – which ones would I be happy to relax?

Am I using my values merely to keep me in my comfort zone?

Do my team's values differ from those of the overall organisation?

Who and what are influencing changes in values?

Is anything stopping me influencing the organisation's values?

"Look, if you hold it <u>this</u> way up."

Notes

Notes

2. How do I measure success?

Why ask myself this question?

By defining 'success' in the first place, I have a goal to aim for.

To help prepare for further success.

To understand my organisational context: am I answering to the owners, the directors, the leading managers or other stakeholders?

Are there common measures of success?

Are these being measured and recognised?

Consider also questions: 11, 58, 59

References:
1. Goodhart's Law - *"When a measure becomes a target, it ceases to be a good measure."*
2. Drucker - *"What gets measured gets managed."*

What insights might I expect to gain?

How do I balance 'success' in this area of my life with all the other areas I inhabit?

Am I measuring what is important or what is possible to measure? (Am I focused on doing the right things rather than doing things right?)

If success is 'ours', then have I ensured that 'we' have all agreed on the scale and the calibration? Is more dialogue needed to agree measures of success?

Do our actions and behaviours show that we really understand what success is?

What do I want to be remembered for?

3. Do I understand why the people at the top are in their position?

Why ask myself this question?

The better to understand what it takes to be successful in my organisation and whether I am prepared to 'do what it takes'.

Consider also questions: 33, 56, 68

References:
1. *The Prince* by Niccolo Machiavelli (Penguin Classics, 2011)

What insights might I expect to gain?

To understand more easily the values and culture of my organisation:

"The halls of fame are open wide and they are always full; some go in by the door called 'push', and some by the door called 'pull'."

Are the people in the top positions the real influencers? Do their achievements justify their formal roles? What would they say? How might their responses help me to achieve my goals and those of the organisation?

The higher up the organisational ladder people get, the more important emotional intelligence becomes. Yet promotion is often the result of being more competent than anyone else in one's previous role.

The role of the chief executive, with regard to the top team, is to teach, tolerate or terminate; has the most appropriate one for each member been adopted?

4. What would I prefer that others did not know?

Why ask myself this question?

To uncover what I am sweeping under the carpet.

To face up to weaknesses and sensitivities I may be concealing, perhaps even from myself.

To identify difficult conversations I am avoiding.

To retain control over difficult conversations that I am not ready to have.

To be able properly to shield particular individuals (or the whole team) from uncertainties that would trouble them, but where the outcome is not theirs to influence.

Consider also questions: 54, 82, 83

References:
1. The Johari window: http://en.wikipedia.org/wiki/Johari_window

What insights might I expect to gain?

Do I trust my colleagues? Am I being overprotective?
Am I courageous enough to share my weaknesses as
well as my strengths?

What are the alternatives? What would be the worst
outcome if I choose to do nothing? Even if I can trust
my team, information leaks and I need to consider
what would be the ramifications, elsewhere in the
organisation and with external stakeholders.

How can I expose my vulnerabilities in a positive
way which does not damage our effectiveness as a
team or my position as a leader?

The leader's role is to remove potential problems,
not sweep them under the carpet.

5. What do I see over the horizon that others have not seen?

Why ask myself this question?

In our 'conceptual' age, I must be able to lead myself to flourish. Leaders see further and wider than others.

Be better prepared to respond to change that cannot be predicted.

My unique perspective enables me to scan parts of the horizon not visible to others. Am I making that ability available to the rest of my team?

Answering this challenging question might greatly improve my team's performance.

It is unlikely that my perspective is the same as the rest of the team's. I should keep asking myself this question until I come up with an answer and then find the right opportunity to present it.

Consider also questions: 46, 47, 74

References:
1. Elina Hiltunen - *Good Sources of Weak Signals*
2. John Hagel III, John Seely Brown and Lang Davison - *Shaping Strategy in a World of Constant Disruption*
3. Institute of Future
4. School of International Futures
5. *The Core Competence of a Corporation* by Prahalad & Hamel (Harvard Business Review, 1990)
6. *Contemporary Strategy Analysis* by R.M. Grant (Wiley & Sons, 2012)
7. *Releasing Your Potential* by Myles Monrow (Destiny Image, 2007)

What insights might I expect to gain?

Becoming aware of my unique perspective and how it might be best appreciated by my team, particularly in relation to opportunities and threats.

I may detect early signals that my environment is changing.

Or perhaps I may have been holding back for reasons of habit, comfort or self-interest, which should be overcome.

(There is no need to see clearly over the horizon, just to alert others to what I think I see, like a good lookout. They can decide its significance.)

Notes

Notes

6. What is the most searching question I could ask now?

Why ask myself this question?

It's all too easy to allow habitual thinking to produce answers to strategic questions that may increasingly be inappropriate.

Finding the right questions to ask is more difficult than arriving at an answer.

Only I can identify the most important question for myself now.

Selecting the question will indicate my current most important concern.

I might use the answer to bring about improvement.

Consider also questions: all

References:
1. The US Military Decision Making Process (MDMO)

What insights might I expect to gain?

I may uncover an underlying assumption that may be holding me or my team back.

One of the roles of a leader is to challenge 'group think'.

Remember Kipling's six serving men: What and Why and When and How and Where and Who.

The most searching question may be difficult to pose and the answer uncertain.

Further reflection may help me decide whether I have selected the most important question, or the simplest to answer and to whom it is most important, me or my team.

7. What do I do when the behaviour of others clashes with policies, procedures or cultures?

Why ask myself this question?

To examine the balance between being frozen by red tape and an individualistic approach that disregards corporate guidelines.

My actions send stronger signals than any amount of talk.

Turning a blind eye does not mean others do not see what has occurred.

Formal policies, procedures and culture need leadership and reinforcement.

Consider also questions: 61, 83, 90

What insights might I expect to gain?

There are a small number of principles about how to behave which are fundamental and they should be internalised; contrast with tick box mentality. Where am I and where are we?

Whether I see these behaviours as opportunities or threats to me or to the organisation? Does it matter? Is it enriching or damaging?

My response indicates whether I am active or passive on this topic, a believer just in top-down management or also in bottom-up, a protector of the status quo or willing to encourage change.

To what extent am I prepared to lose business rather than accede to unacceptable local customs?

Am I sufficiently aware of other's behaviour? To what extent am I going to be responsible for other's behaviour?

Will my actions lead to a more self-sustaining solution?

8. What are the current constraints on growth?

Why ask myself this question?

It forces me to take a helicopter view of the organisation; to look outside my own area.

Growth opportunities often compete for resources with existing business and may lack the necessary political clout.

Constraints can be mindsets, not only resources.

Growth of what? Remember increased turnover is not necessarily profitable and often fails to provide a higher return on capital employed.

To ensure that priority is given to managing the bottlenecks.

Consider also questions: 15, 74, 86

References:
1. E. Goldratt's Theory of Constraints

What insights might I expect to gain?

Potential weaknesses in my business model; this will give me the opportunity to address them.

A budget process that prevents innovation.

I may question what kind of growth we are aiming for, and our investors are expecting: turnover, profits, return on capital, share price, etc.

Is my/our lack of ambition a constraint?

What business am I in?

Are we investing in areas of greatest opportunity? A good check on my strategy.

It may encourage me to see opportunities an external investor would see and that I may not see. Are we at our funding limit, for borrowings, for equity? Will my actions lead to a more self-sustaining solution?

9. How adaptable is my organisation?

Why ask myself this question?

Though we would all like to anticipate change, more often than not, it catches us unawares and we are forced to adapt. Making sure that I, my team and my organisation are able to adapt to external pressure is the next best thing to anticipating change.

How do I keep an open mind? Cultivate curiosity? Find good ideas which can be copied with pride? Keep mentally and organisationally flexible?

To ensure that sub-systems are not optimised at the expense of the whole organisation.

Anticipating barriers will help to surmount them.

Consider also questions: 8, 55, 86

What insights might I expect to gain?

Clarify those things that I do not want to see changed, such as brand values, principles, culture; and those that I am happy to let go of such as location, product portfolio, and distribution channels.

To learn who, including myself, has understood that change is inevitable and has the demonstrated capacity to lead and/or accept continuing change.

To identify the 'energy sappers'.

The extent to which I and my team are attached to our way of doing things might surprise me. Other people's attachment to ideas and habits are easy to spot, not so ours.

10. What proportion of my staff can explain our business model?

Why ask myself this question?

To build awareness of the proportion of people, especially managers, in my organisation who understand what business we are really in.

To identify whether the whole organisation is rowing in the same direction.

How healthy is my organisation? Are we functionally efficient but badly coordinated?

Aligning mental models around the business model is essential for coordinated action.

Attempting to deliver performance or to change the culture, e.g. to move from a not-for-profit to a profit model requires staff to understand and support the new imperatives.

Consider also questions: 17, 22, 52

References:

1. http://www.businessmodelgeneration.com/
   Business Models with Strategy - tools, videos, and an interface that's easy for anybody.

What insights might I expect to gain?

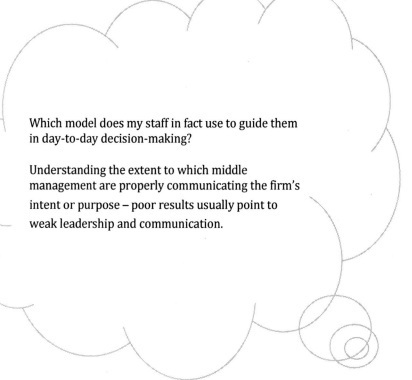

Which model does my staff in fact use to guide them in day-to-day decision-making?

Understanding the extent to which middle management are properly communicating the firm's intent or purpose – poor results usually point to weak leadership and communication.

11. Who are my five key stakeholders?

Why ask myself this question?

They justify my existence and I need to keep close to them.

They should impact my governance.

If I leave any one of them out, I am potentially storing up serious problems.

Lack of focus on my stakeholders may damage my career and hopes of promotion.

Poor communications with them puts me at risk.

With key stakeholders aligned, I greatly increase my chances of success.

Consider also questions: 14, 81, 98

References:
1. https://www.tomorroscompany.com/ The Tomorrow's Company Inquiry report from the RSA published in 1996 identifies an archetypal 'five key stakeholders' and discusses the importance of managing an appropriate balance between their objectives.

What insights might I expect to gain?

There may be surprises when I stand back to answer this question. Maybe I have some blind spots that others can see.

'Squeaky wheels' might distract me from my key stakeholders – whether internal or external.

Have I just listed the usual suspects? Map stakeholders by interest and influence – think STEEPLE for externals: Social, Technical, Economic, Environmental, Political, Legal and Ethical.

"Of course you're not being _FIRED_!
Think of it as a personnel shuffle in which,
unfortunately, you may not have been considered.
— Please clean up your desk and be gone by 6PM."

Notes

Notes

12. Is the spread of length of service of my senior team appropriate?

Why ask myself this question?

To review whether or not my organisation has the right blend of experience and new ideas.

It's important to ensure that my organisation's continuity is provided for as well as is possible through good management succession planning.

Consider also questions: 60, 66, 71

What insights might I expect to gain?

To what extent my business relies on long-term relationships with my customers.

How my organisation stimulates and rewards new thinking.

How blinkered my people are.

Where does my organisation need new thinking and new blood? Can I provide this? How does my organisation integrate it?

Is length of service, in this organisation or the sector, a valid criterion for judging ability to plan for an ever-changing future?

Is there a danger that too many people serving for too long a period may lead to 'group think' and a failure to challenge?

Is there an adequate range of thinking and diversity of opinion?

Where do I need new thinking and the 'new blood' to do it?

How well do I know the aspirations of my key team members?

13. Why does my organisation need a goal other than survival?

Why ask myself this question?

Without a meaningful goal, my organisation will not survive.

Survival is a necessary but not sufficient condition for success.

Survival is not the justification for an organisation's existence.

If all I have to offer is survival, my best people will leave.

I need to justify allocation of current and future resources.

Consider also questions: 2, 20, 31

References:

1. Simon Sinek's Golden Circles; Think about technology S-Curves and life cycles https://www.slideshares.net/Christiansandstrom/technology-s-curves

What insights might I expect to gain?

Ongoing confirmation of the purpose of my organisation.

There is no value added in a survival situation except where I am trying to execute an end of life or exit strategy. So if I am just surviving, I should start planning for the end of my organisation.

Different expectations of the different stakeholders.

A gap between what stakeholders have been promised and what is delivered.

Tensions between owners and employees.

14. Who is really my boss?

Why ask myself this question?

Of course, 'the customer is king', but the larger my organisation, the more indirect my access to the customer becomes, and the more I have to balance the influence of different stakeholders.

Unless I think through my formal, informal, stakeholder and personal reporting relationships, I will never be able to perform in my role.

I have to survive formal appraisals but must not think this is anything more than preparing for my exit.

Progression happens as a result of tiny differences in widely perceived superior performance.

Building trusted relationships with the centres of power in my organisation is essential.

Consider also questions: 159, 64, 93

References:

1. '10 rules for managing your boss'. http://www.rediff.com/money/2005/aug/12spec/htm

What insights might I expect to gain?

I may be reporting to one person, but being influenced by another/others.

In complex modern organisations, annual reviews increasingly take into account the views of colleagues as well as the person I formally report to. Ignore them at your peril.

Who would I like my next boss to be?

15. What is the unique competence of my organisation?

Why ask myself this question?

It's the reason my company exists.

If we cannot readily establish what our unique competencies are, we are doomed.

Caring for this uniqueness reduces risk and helps me to know what to protect.

Maintains focus on our brand.

Core competencies are central to competitive advantage.

Consider also questions: 22, 81, 92

References:

1. A core competency is a concept in management theory originally advocated by C.K. Prahalad and Gary Hamel.

What insights might I expect to gain?

It may reveal confusion and conflicting views.

We may not be taking the best advantage of this competence.

We may not be communicating it clearly.

The degree to which our unique competence is valued by our customers.

Reveals confusion, in-house or externally.

If I intend to compete in a market, the first step is to identify the core competencies I will need. Then I can make an objective comparison and examine the options for their availability. Failure to do this has led to multiple billion dollar losses in apparently well-managed businesses.

Ask my best customer, 'What do our competitors say about us?' What then?

16. How do I ensure the welfare of my team?
Why ask myself this question?

Achieving success requires a balance of different elements, one of which, most often ignored, is the welfare of the team.

Getting the right balance between a focus on doing the job, the needs of individuals and my team is the primary role of the leader.

If I want to get the best people on my team, it has to be a team that people want to join.

And if I have the best people, I need to look after them or they will join another team.

Set priorities and ensure that every successful step is celebrated. Stand up for my team.

Consider also questions: 36, 72, 99

References:
1. See John Adair's action-centred leadership
   http://www.businessballs.com/action.htm

What insights might I expect to gain?

My assumptions about people and their motivations may be wrong.

People will have competencies and needs that I never knew about and that can be shared.

If I help uncover them at the beginning of forming a team, the performance of the team will be hugely improved.

What it takes to sustain the welfare of the team – a team-building day at the start of the project is hardly sufficient.

"I'm sorry, I can't help. Even a lifetime of contemplative meditation hasn't made me able to understand PROFIT AND LOSS."

Notes

Notes

17. How can I ensure that everyone understands the profit and loss statement?

Why ask myself this question?

Many operational people focus on achieving gross margins because fixed overheads are out of their control, whereas net profitability of the organisation is what defines their success.

It will make my people realise the importance of costs that lie outside their function, e.g. there is no point in selling if sales do not make a contribution.

People should be measured and rewarded for their contribution to the profit of the whole organisation, not only for matters within their own control.

Consider also questions: 10, 18, 43

References:

1. *The Accounting Game: Basic Accounting Fresh from the Lemonade Stand* by Darrell Mullis and Judith Orloss (Sourcebooks, 1998)

What insights might I expect to gain?

I will realise how few people really understand how the business operates and the relationship between the different elements of the profit and loss account.

If purchasing focuses only on the cost of materials at the exclusion of quality and manufacturing costs, then the overall product profitability will be severely impacted.

If sales teams are allowed to focus on revenue and gross margin without an awareness of product net profitability, then I could have a very busy company making no money.

"Really, what I'd recommend is that you should have used a different bank to begin with."

Notes

Notes

18. What is the first thing I could do to improve cash flow?
Why ask myself this question?

I may have a profitable business but go out of business because I do not have any money.

Cash, not profit, keeps me in business.

Cash is related to my balance sheet, profit is related to the profit and loss account.

It will release cash that will allow me to make strategic investments for growth.

Consider also questions: 8, 9, 38

What insights might I expect to gain?

It will show me how good I am at delivering my strategic plan.

It will show me the resilience of my organisation in the face of risk.

If I need to rely on other people's money, I will lose control of my business.

It makes me realise how good we are at debtor and creditor control.

19. How would my people know I love them?

Why ask myself this question?

If my people don't know that I love them, then they will assume I don't – nobody can lead an organisation if people fear you or are indifferent.

It is the fastest way to develop trust. When people trust you, they will follow you.

I may not like all my people, but I can certainly love them.

If I love my people, I accept them for everything that they are and this is crucial to building a team that delivers.

The more you love your area of expertise – medicine, accountancy, law, etc. – the more you excel at it. Managers' area of expertise is people.

Consider also questions: 16, 72, 99

What insights might I expect to gain?

How I reacted when I saw the word 'love' in this question. What does it say about me?

Powerful emotions, properly engaged, make a huge difference to people's willingness to engage.

It's about time the traditional organisational pyramid is inverted. Leaders need to support the people rather than command them.

How I support my people.

Love is not about what you think but how you feel, and how you feel is what you communicate to people. It needs to be authentic; you can't 'fake it till you make it' with this one.

20. What would I like my legacy to be?

Why ask myself this question?

It will make me think of the even longer term. Perhaps I can include things like social impact and contribution, which can be an important part of developing a highly-motivated team.

There are many examples of short-term focus having damaging consequences on the organisation's long-term interest.

Consider also questions: 53, 58, 95

References:

1. John Kay's report on 'Short-termism in the City'
   http://www.publications.parliament.uk/pa/cm201313/cmselect/cmbis/603/603.pdf

What insights might I expect to gain?

A better understanding of how easy it is to lose focus on the long term as I deal with the never ending flow of short-term problems.

I might get more meaningful answers to my question, 'What's it all about?'

Understanding if there is a need to challenge the appropriateness of the current culture.

"Latest research shows that over 138.3% of people manipulate statistics to prove their point!"

Notes

Notes

21. How do I know I am being told the truth?
Why ask myself this question?

I can never be sure, but I need to understand if there are areas where the likelihood might be high.

To make me realise that everything I receive from others will inevitably be biased.

It's important to calibrate the biases.

Dictators usually fall to a palace 'coup'. I should ensure I have access to a wide range of diverse and objective opinions.

I may be misleading others and making bad decisions myself.

To assess the level of trust in my network.

Consider also questions: 59, 61, 82

References:
1. The small boy and the story of the Emperor's New Clothes; King Cnut disproving his flatterers as the tide came in; Shakespeare: Henry V - the night before Agincourt.

What insights might I expect to gain?

If I am not aware, someone else might really be running the company.

Have I a reputation for shooting messengers who bring me bad news?

An understanding of the level of trust in my network.

My communications may not be influencing my people.

I should consider more carefully the motivation of those reporting to me.

I do not have available the expertise to know the answer.

I rely too much on audits and not enough on honest reporting.

I may have lost control.

22. Which three adjectives would I use to describe both success and failure in my organisation?

Why ask myself this question?

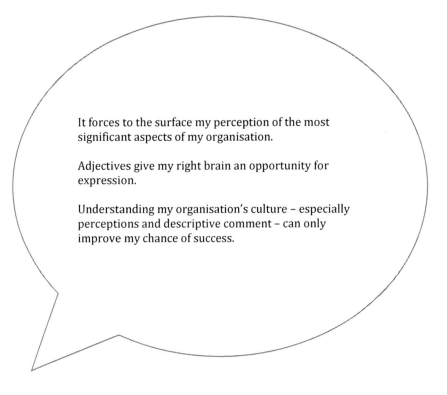

It forces to the surface my perception of the most significant aspects of my organisation.

Adjectives give my right brain an opportunity for expression.

Understanding my organisation's culture – especially perceptions and descriptive comment – can only improve my chance of success.

Consider also questions: 15, 29

References:
1. *Why Countries Fail? The End of Ethics* E. Roosevelt

What insights might I expect to gain?

There is a difference between quantitative measures and the reasons for achieving them.

Many aspects of an organisation's culture cannot be expressed in numbers, yet the culture will enable or defeat our rational tactics.

Are these the adjectives my colleagues would use?

To see if our failures are the opposite of our successes.

Test – are these genuinely my adjectives, or are they borrowed from others?

To become a learning organisation, we need to build on our successes and avoid our failures.

"I'm sorry Sir. What constitutes an 'Act of God' is _clearly_ laid out in your insurance policy agreement."

Notes

Notes

23. Do I need more external advice?

Why ask myself this question?

It is always worth questioning whether the information I rely on continues to be good enough for the challenges that lie ahead.

To uncover areas where I don't feel confident.

To help me assess the extent to which my internal sources are up-to-date, reliable and unbiased.

Consider also questions: 46, 83, 93

What insights might I expect to gain?

Am I humble enough to ask for advice? Asking for advice is not a sign of weakness – neither does it mean that I have to take it! But I will certainly take a better informed decision as a consequence of obtaining it.

My degree of confidence in my decision-making process.

Are there known unknowns...?

Am I matching the demands of an uncertain external environment and the internal competence of the organisation?

Today's success is no guarantee of future survival; anticipating future needs is an important survival capability. Outsiders may have better insights.

My fear of hearing something I would rather avoid may become obvious.

"Retraining CEOs is a complete nightmare."

Notes

Notes

24. Could I use a mentor or coach?

Why ask myself this question?

To prevent myself from slipping into complacency.

I may be setting too low a bar for myself and my organisation.

Having someone to turn to who is impartial and external to the organisation could help me navigate a difficult passage.

Further improvement of my performance may not be possible if I just rely on my own judgement and goal setting.

Consider also questions: 59, 73, 83

What insights might I expect to gain?

It reveals how much appetite I really have for continuous learning, readiness to be challenged, impartial feedback.

Whether I would really be prepared to act on the outcomes if I took on a mentor or coach and set myself goals that I do not follow up.

Am I prepared to expose my vulnerabilities?

Growing isolated may be a difficult situation to recognise without a mentor or coach.

25. Which organisation do I most admire?

Why ask myself this question?

To understand the attributes that I admire in an organisation: could there be something we can copy?

To compare and contrast these attributes with those of my own organisation.

To have a benchmark and an icon that can be recognised by my team.

To help me step back and look at my organisation dispassionately as an outsider would.

Consider also questions: 30, 70, 92

What insights might I expect to gain?

I may recognise that the grass might be greener on my side of the fence.

Clarification of the operational and/or leadership gap between my organisation and the one I admire.

An understanding of what has been frustrating me; what I need to do and where to start.

26. What astonishes me most about my organisation?

Why ask myself this question?

Once I have spent time in an organisation, I may cease to see its competences and begin to take it for granted.

The real stars in my organisation may not be readily visible.

Investigating what we have may lead to all sorts of surprising discoveries – good and bad.

Standing back to answer this question may start conversations leading to strengthening performance.

Consider also questions: 15, 46, 96

References:

1. *The Talented Manager: 67 Gems of Business Wisdom* by A Furnham (Palgrave Macmillan, 2012)

What insights might I expect to gain?

Astonishment supposes some disconnect between perception and reality.

Astonishment can be an early insight; early insights can lead to early actions.

If I am astonished by something, this could reveal a whole new opportunity for the organisation.

To check whether I take too many things for granted.

Am I in touch with what is happening in my organisation?

27. Do I take all my annual leave?

Why ask myself this question?

It will reveal how responsible I am in taking care of myself and my other responsibilities (family, direct reports, etc.).

To compare my behaviour with that required of all staff. Am I a good example?

I need to take stock periodically of my work/life balance.

Consider also questions: 41, 53, 73

References:
1. *Rogue Trader* by N. Leeson (Sphere, 2015)

What insights might I expect to gain?

I may discover that I secretly think I am indispensable. Is this a view that is shared? Am I putting my organisation at risk?

I may have difficulty delegating. Is this because I don't trust my team or I don't trust myself?

I may be afraid of finding unexpected and unpleasant changes on my return.

What I am avoiding by not taking all my annual leave.

Whether or not I plan my work and my private life with the same imperatives in mind.

28. When on holiday, how often do I access my emails?

Why ask myself this question?

To prepare for my holiday by ensuring that others can handle what I consider important and urgent.

It helps me to categorise situations that are of high importance and urgent, which should be very few, and those that I want my team to handle.

Forcing people who are standing in for me to deal with the rest of the work both helps them to grow and gives me insight into their potential.

Consider also questions: 1, 41, 97

References:

1. Ilan-mochari - *An Introvert's Guide to Surviving a Holiday Party*

What insights might I expect to gain?

It is always important to remember that I am not my role.

The value of getting my team to understand what is important for them to do.

Do I feel anxious about not being 'in control'?

Am I setting an appropriate example to my team? Do I email them when they are on holiday?

Am I doing a proper job in developing my team? (And do I have the right people on my team?)

29. I am in a coffee shop and start talking to a stranger. I am asked what my organisation does. Can I answer this in 30 seconds such that the stranger says 'tell me more'?

Why ask myself this question?

Knowing how to answer this question is fundamental to the success of every organisation. I should ask myself this whenever I start a new activity.

This is about clarity of purpose and the value that my organisation adds.

That there is something in it for the stranger by learning more.

Consider also questions: 30, 74, 96

References:

1. *Ogilvy, D* - "On the average, five times as many people read the headline as read the body copy. When you have written your headline, you have spent eighty cents of your dollar." [known as the 'elevator pitch']
2. Otis, E (1853) - "All safe gentlemen. All safe!"

What insights might I expect to gain?

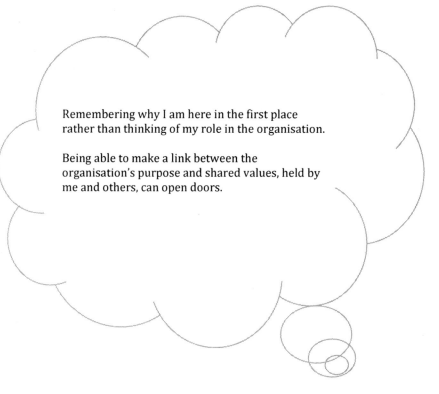

Remembering why I am here in the first place rather than thinking of my role in the organisation.

Being able to make a link between the organisation's purpose and shared values, held by me and others, can open doors.

"I hereby sentence you to life imprisonment as an accounts manager at a mid-size suburban paper merchants."

Notes

Notes

30. Why am I proud of the organisation for which I work?

Why ask myself this question?

Feeling I have shared in an achievement that I believe to be worthwhile.

To help me help my people find their motivation when energy is low.

Pride in what I do, and for whom, is an important aspect of being happy at work. Happy workers are more productive workers.

Consider also questions: 1, 84, 96

What insights might I expect to gain?

If I am not proud of my organisation, then I need to question why I work for it.

Seeing the big picture and believing in it helps me and my people to understand why our part of it is important.

Values only permeate when they are shared. How do I ensure that everyone is able to work with the values they support?

I may find new reasons for loving the work I do.

31. What would the world be like without my organisation?

Why ask myself this question?

It helps me to be realistic about the unique contribution that we make.

To be sustainable, the goods or services that an organisation produces need to be valued by the outside world.

Is being part of a sustainable organisation important to me?

When I am too successful, I start thinking that the world owes me; I need to put my importance into perspective.

To understand in whose interest my organisation is operating.

To remind myself of what my organisation really contributes to society – the people it employs, the service it provides, how our clients are better off with us in the world.

Consider also questions: 15, 29, 81

What insights might I expect to gain?

The question will prompt me to carefully consider the contribution that my organisation makes to society. It will remind me of how many people my organisation touches.

Do I understand and agree with what my organisation contributes to the world/society?

Through the fellowship and associations of my organisation, I can leverage the impact of my ideals in creating a better world.

Sometimes an organisation has fulfilled its purpose but still lives on.

What might my organisation do to create an even better world?

What do others say about the value of my organisation in the world/society?

32. If I were the sole owner of my organisation, what one thing would I change?

Why ask myself this question?

It helps me to focus on what is really important.

Knowing what I would like to change may allow me to take advantage of opportunities when they arise.

If I see clearly what needs to change and I champion it, I will probably succeed despite the lack of formal authority.

Differences between an owner's and a manager's goals, without careful attention to their consequences, may lead to dysfunctional organisations.

Consider also questions: 5, 47, 58

What insights might I expect to gain?

The things that frustrate me and that I am
powerless to change.

The expectations owners may have of the
management of the company.

Understanding the market value now and in the
future may affect the choice of strategy that seems
most appropriate for meeting my personal
objectives.

The relationship between owners and managers is
increasingly coloured by differences in goals.
Thinking of each other's priorities provides
opportunities to respect other's needs.

33. Who are the influencers in my organisation?

Why ask myself this question?

If I want to get things done, I need to know who can help me.

In organisations, the informal power structure is more influential than might be expected.

Failure to consider influencers is a common reason for the failure of change programmes.

Consider also questions: 38, 45, 93

References:
1. *The Invisible Organisation,* Neil Farmer (Gower, 2008)

What insights might I expect to gain?

How I distinguish between influence and office politics.

If I find out who talks to whom, I can establish what informal relationships exist and how I can use them.

Whether I know what influence I have and how well I use it.

I may be ignoring people who have influence.

I may be being ignored.

Notes

Notes

34. Imagine that consultants have fairy dust that they can sprinkle over your organisation to change it in any way you want. What would you like it to do for yours?

Why ask myself this question?

In order to make improvements, I have to 'think differently' and break with precedent.

Without new thinking, my organisation cannot develop. External advisers can often see a wider perspective and therefore challenge my current thinking.

Starting with a radical question like this can free up my thinking.

"Insanity is doing the same thing over and over again but expecting different results."
Rita Mae Brown

Consider also questions: 53, 55, 74

What insights might I expect to gain?

It is helpful sometimes to force myself to think radically in order to escape from normal patterns and instinctive inhibitions.

Playing this mental game can help me to make radical changes for the better – or, by coming from an unexpected angle, find some practical steps I can take now.

The question also forces me to think seriously about what I really want my organisation to achieve, without focusing on current challenges or barriers – or using these as an excuse to do nothing.

35. When something goes wrong, how do I know if it's important?

Why ask myself this question?

It forces me to distinguish between the urgent and the important.

It keeps me aligned with our long and short-term strategies.

I have to find the few important mistakes that, if corrected, will lead my organisation to succeed. The Pareto principle states that, for many events, roughly 80% of the effects come from 20% of the causes.

Understanding why things go wrong is the first step towards their correction. If I trace the original cause or causes, this will help me to evaluate the impact of the error and whether it is one of the important 20%.

Consider also questions: 21, 62, 82

What insights might I expect to gain?

I may uncover any misalignment between problem-solving and strategy.

Whether we are all taking the path of least resistance instead of addressing the important issues.

Identifying important mistakes and their causes will lead me to important learning for future decision-taking and to what is really important on the path to achieving our goals.

This analysis should not be used to apportion blame but to decide what process changes I might make in my organisation, how my team could be developed and what matters I could delegate for resolution elsewhere.

If I don't understand the importance of things that go wrong, then I will not understand my organisation's processes or their intended outcomes.

"What exactly is your problem with my filing system?"

Notes

Notes

36. What do I do to demonstrate that I take feedback seriously?

Why ask myself this question?

Receiving and giving open, honest and robust feedback is an indication of a relationship based on trust.

Do I act upon the feedback that I receive or just pay lip service to it?

Because I want people to take the feedback I give them seriously.

If I don't demonstrate that I take feedback seriously, I am indicating that I am not open to feedback in the future.

Consider also questions: 82, 88, 99

What insights might I expect to gain?

To what extent I value the views of those with whom I work.

Am I truly a team player?

Whether I really want to change for the better.

Am I avoiding giving and requesting feedback? If so, why might that be?

37. How do my actions support the culture of my organisation?

Why ask myself this question?

Culture binds an organisation together; being at odds with the culture will be uncomfortable, both for me and the organisation.

By aligning my actions with the culture of the organisation, I shall be seen as a supportive member; the opposite is also true.

How do I truly identify with my organisation's culture?

Our stakeholders, not least staff and customers, support the organisation because of the culture: I cannot let them down.

Sometimes it is necessary to challenge my culture and/or my organisation's culture.

Consider also questions: 7, 64, 90

What insights might I expect to gain?

A better understanding of my organisation's culture and my degree of comfort with it.

If my actions are not supportive of my organisation's culture, I may gain a better insight into the reasons why.

To comply, I need to be conscious of my actions and how they might be perceived. Similarly, for my team members.

If I can't identify with the culture of my organisation then I might need to consider working for another organisation.

Do I have any colleagues who are also at odds with the organisation's culture? Am I the only person out of place, or is the organisation dysfunctional?

Have I communicated my understanding of the culture to all those for whose actions I am responsible, and listened to their responses?

(—— "You're fired!!")
"Well you could _try_ firing me and keeping my intellectual property, but I just don't think it'll work."

Notes

38. How does innovation happen in my organisaton?
Why ask myself this question?

Organisations need to innovate (people, processes, and products) in order to survive in the longer term.

Innovation can be part of an organisation's culture; I need to understand how we are fostering it through formal and informal processes.

To understand the contribution I am making to these processes – or how my behaviour blocks or limits innovation.

Innovation may be espoused by my organisation, but is this 'real'?

Consider also questions: 8, 88, 98

What insights might I expect to gain?

How innovation is positively encouraged, formally or informally, in my organisation. Are there any constraints upon innovation?

Whether innovation is important to me/my organisation. Do I have a part to play in innovation?

What our organisational approach is to innovation – breakthrough thinking or incremental change?

How my organisation recognises the importance of innovation; is this linked to its subsequent exploitation?

How important it is to me that innovation is valued in the organisation for which I work.

What examples of innovation have occurred over the past two or three years and how they were achieved?

39. What are the first three things I would suggest my successor reviews?

Why ask myself this question?

It may help me to identify things that I am unable to do but which my organisation needs to have done.

Failure to act on these things will be extremely damaging over the long term. It is possible that my team knows about these issues and is unhappy I have not acted.

This question can help with succession planning, which is very important – and is also a valuable way to get a new perspective on what I should be prioritising, planning and doing.

Consider also questions: 15, 74, 92

References:

1. See *Powerful Conversations*
   http://www.youtube.com/watch?v=veKvJHCkvmU

What insights might I expect to gain?

A better understanding of what my priorities should be if I depersonalise my thinking and escape from my personal and emotional ties.

Am I really, really sure I cannot take action myself? Why haven't I already addressed these issues?

Am I focusing on what is really important for the organisation or on what is urgent?

Can I distinguish between doing what I like to do and what the organisation really needs to have done?

40. What would be the consequences if I took three months off?

Why ask myself this question?

Like everyone, I quite naturally want to believe that I am indispensable.

If I truly am indispensable, then this could be a risk, both to me and the organisation.

How could both I and the organisation benefit from the new perspectives that my absence from the day-to-day routine would enable?

The unexpected can always happen – have I thought through the consequences?

Consider also questions: 20, 51, 64

What insights might I expect to gain?

Ask myself why there would be no risk or a considerable risk.

If I am truly indispensable in my current role, then I may never be promoted.

I may not be delegating sufficiently, both to my own detriment and to those who report to me.

Am I merely delegating or am I developing the leadership abilities of my team members?

How I could use my absence to develop the capacities and capabilities of my key reports?

Is my work/life balance acceptable?

Do I want others to see me as invaluable – am I insecure and, if so, why?

Do others think that I am indispensable? Is this a source of pride or concern?

41. Am I a workaholic or do I just love my job?

Why ask myself this question?

There's nothing wrong with loving my job unless this becomes obsessive.

Spending too much time at work can cause stress not only to me but also to my family and friends.

To determine what example I am setting for my colleagues.

How can I contribute to growing the business further if I am already over capacity?

Understanding why I spend so much time at work may help me to understand better my work/life balance.

What do I understand my job to be?

Consider also questions: 40, 63, 73, 85

What insights might I expect to gain?

What I might be avoiding by spending so much time at work.

Am I devoid of interests outside work? Am I boring socially?

Are my work and life happily balanced?

How might I be able to share the pleasures I see in my job so that others obtain similar satisfaction?

Honestly understanding the difference, for me, between being a workaholic and loving my job can help me to achieve a better work/life balance.

Am I using the fact that I love my job as an excuse for long hours and absence from my family/friends? Or am I using an unhappy/unfulfilling personal life as an excuse to be a workaholic?

42. What would cause me to consider leaving my job or changing careers?

Why ask myself this question?

I need to be aware of the personal and organisational factors that originally led me to my job and whether these are still valid.

As careers become more fragmented and flexible, it is important to be clear about my underlying motivations and how my current role and organisation satisfy these.

Leaving my job or changing career is always a personal option. I need to understand when to consider exercising that option.

Consider also questions: 53, 76, 78

What insights might I expect to gain?

Greater clarity about my priorities in life and the impact of changes over time.

Understand which organisational, professional and personal factors are really important to me rather than to the organisation.

The 'push' factors which might drive me from my current role and the 'pull' factors which might draw me to another role or organisation.

How bad would things have to get for me to quit or become a whistleblower?

43. How much time do I allow my people for training and personal development?

Why ask myself this question?

Developing people is, arguably, my most important job as a leader.

My influence in my organisation will be highly dependent on the development that I can offer to my people.

Is development seen as a personal or an organisational responsibility in my organisation – or shared?

Long-term improvements in relevant competencies are key to a thriving, adaptive organisation with highly motivated people.

Consider also questions: 10, 16, 60

What insights might I expect to gain?

Giving individual development a high priority leads to the improved competence and future resilience of my organisation.

Aspiration to undertake development programmes is a powerful management tool.

Would I be willing to invest in my own development if my company did not have the resources to do so?

"My chief executive doesn't believe that 'TUMMY RUBS' and 'WALKIES' are not sufficient remuneration for his years of service."

Notes

Notes

44. How do I encourage value from our non-executives?

Why ask myself this question?

Good non-executives usually want to add value but may need my help to fulfil their role.

We can all become introspective – it's a safe place to be! By listening to others, and thereby testing my views, I can gain confidence in any decisions that I may make.

Non-executives can too readily be intimidated by the executive and vice versa.

Non-executives should bring an extra and external objective view of an organisation.

In not using non-executives, I could be missing a valuable opportunity.

Consider also questions: 48, 65, 93

What insights might I expect to gain?

I may have concerns about the gaps in my knowledge and haven't considered how non-executives could help me.

I may not have thought about what skills and experience exist within the non-executives and how to leverage them.

I may find a valuable coach or mentor for myself amongst the non-executives.

I may not have taken or created opportunities to interact with the non-executives.

How willing I am to listen to, and perhaps learn from, external views.

45. How should I target the 'right' customers, internal and external?

Why ask myself this question?

It will make me consider who the 'right' customers are for my organisation. What makes them right? Is it that they are demanding, thus keeping us ahead of the competition? Is it that they are profitable? Have they become our product development partners?

This is more easily done in smaller rather than larger organisations where customers are more rightly regarded as stakeholders.

Business process re-engineering introduced the idea of internal customers: we are all part of a business process and the input we need for our work comes from either an external or internal customer. Are they the right customers or are we confusing our processes?

Understanding who my 'right' customers are and what core and supporting processes I need to serve them effectively is fundamental to my organisation's success.

Consider also questions: 11, 96, 98

What insights might I expect to gain?

Understanding who the right customers are for my organisation will provide clarity in both strategic and tactical dimensions.

However, not all customers are important and it is critical for me to understand the relative importance of my customers.

Understanding, specifying and developing services to meet customer needs is the functional task of marketing, but effectively running the business processes that serve my customers is the task of the whole team.

Showing that I want to understand my customers builds a strong relationship with them.

Understanding my organisation's processes and operations will enable me to satisfy customers' wishes on a basis that also meets my organisation's criteria.

Asking myself this question may help me to understand better the degree to which my efforts are aligned with my organisation's strategy.

46. To which uncertainty affecting my organisation would I most like the answer?

Why ask myself this question?

To make me focus on my most significant hope or worry, whether internal or external.

It may lead to new initiatives that address the uncertainty.

Reflecting upon this question helps to avoid complacency; am I being an 'ostrich'?

Consider also questions: 8, 31, 48

What insights might I expect to gain?

There might be a major issue that has not been exposed and for which support and contingency plans are inadequate.

The first glib answer may well be replaced by a more fundamental answer after further consideration and self-questioning.

The value of using a scanning template such as, for example, SWOT and/or PESTLE

47. Looking back from three years into the future, what three things did we do to achieve the success we had planned?

Why ask myself this question?

Perhaps the most difficult task facing me is to try and set a vision of the future for my organisation, known as foresight. Success in team games and politics has now been observed in those who can get their team to focus only on success and never on failure.

Achievement motivation theory is the idea that an individual has needs including a need for achievement (the other two being the need for affiliation and power). Those who have a 'need to achieve' are very different from those who have a 'need to avoid failure'.

Asking this question gives me a better understanding of our future and helps me to focus on the key initiatives to achieve it.

Consider also questions: 45, 75, 92

What insights might I expect to gain?

The importance of beginning with the 'end' in mind; in this case also with the 'how' in mind.

Providing me with some of the key elements for success in the future.

Provide the basis for a positive vision that I can use to achieve motivation in my team.

Adopting visioning techniques from leading economic and social forecasters.

48. Looking back from three years into the future, everything has gone terribly for our organisation. What did I fail to do?

Why ask myself this question?

Visualisation, which is also known as mental imagery and rehearsal, is widely used in sports psychology. It improves my quality of decision-making, increases my power of concentration and helps to reduce the pressures of competition while at the same time improving my confidence.

Foresight as to the future of my organisation is one of the primary tasks of the leader.

To force me to consider potential reasons for failure and not just success, though failure should never be used as an opportunity to apportion blame but to learn and improve performance.

Just as success is down to me and the team, so is failure. Realisation of this gives me and my team control over our future.

Consider also questions: 46, 75, 79

What insights might I expect to gain?

How using visualisation techniques have proved successful for sports champions from rugby union to golf.

I may realise I forget to ask of myself and my team "What would it take to...?" as we did not do what was required.

I can understand better where failure might occur either through misguided action or through inaction and whether the causes of failure are likely to be serendipitous or systemic.

When I think of failure, I think of attribution theory. When I win it's natural to attribute this success to myself and the team for playing well, and when I lose I should blame the same people as I did for winning, as we are in control and it is no one else's fault but our own. This gives me a sense of control over what I do.

49. What one thing could the Government do that would help us to succeed?

Why ask myself this question?

To consider the context in which my organisation is required to operate.

To focus on a key driver of my organisation's success that we, alone, are unable to influence.

To ensure that my organisation doesn't simply 'blame the Government' for any impediment to its success.

Consider also questions: 46, 74, 86

What insights might I expect to gain?

Gaining greater clarity about aspects of my organisation's business model that the Government can change or enhance as opposed to those over which it has no control.

Identifying how my organisation can gain advantage over competitors who labour under the same constraints.

Considering how best my organisation might bring influence to bear with Government or those better placed to lobby; identifying if I can do anything to assist.

What could my trade association or professional body do that I alone cannot do?

Identifying what competitors are doing in this area – are they ahead of the game?

Is the existence of, or lack of, a Government policy hindering my organisation's progress?

50. I am now the chief executive of my organisation: what two things will I do immediately?

Why ask myself this question?

Many of the questions in this book are pushing me to think about the purpose of my organisation and the plans that I should formulate for achieving success.

However, it is vital that, as the leader, I demonstrate that I can change plans into action.

In every organisation there are irritating things that can be fixed quickly for relatively low cost. If I commit myself to doing a few of these things, it will have an immediate impact on the organisation and demonstrate that things are going to change.

Making such changes happen ensures that I meet stakeholders' expectations and communicate my intentions clearly as a leader.

Consider also questions: 3, 44, 70

What insights might I expect to gain?

Appreciating that just doing things may be the right course of action – I can't spend all my life asking questions.

An understanding of the small things that are bothering the organisation.

Set the direction and show that I am prepared to act as the leader.

51. How would I brief a person who is replacing me for a few months about this 'issue'?

Why ask myself this question?

To help me stand back and view the 'issue' in perspective.

To understand why this 'issue' is particularly important.

To help me to identify short-term concerns and priorities in the context of continuity.

To focus on the big issues.

To separate the urgent from the important.

Consider also questions: 11, 52, 65

What insights might I expect to gain?

Identify the core elements of the 'issue'.

Understand why, if I can give away this issue for three months, I can't do so permanently?

If I can delegate, then can colleagues also do so?

Helping with my own succession planning by identifying who is capable, plus any recruitment and development needs.

Think what someone who knows me really well would say.

"What do you mean 'IS YOUR PROBLEM URGENT OR IMPORTANT'?'

Notes

Notes

52. How do I set, use and communicate priorities?

Why ask myself this question?

To set priorities and make the best use of time.

Addressing priorities covering both home and work helps lead to a more balanced life.

Getting my priorities clearly set should lead to less stress, both for me and for others impacted.

To have a rationale behind my prioritisation.

My priorities may not be understood by others.

Consider also questions: 5, 73, 85

What insights might I expect to gain?

Understanding if my priorities align with the objectives that I've been set.

Gaining greater certainty that, both at home and at work, others understand my priorities.

Seeing if I am doing what I prefer to do rather than what I need to do.

Writing a 'to do' list can be very therapeutic – but is valueless unless I follow it and in a logical manner!

By taking into account the expressed requirements of others, ensuring that we are all working to the same priorities.

53. What is my unfulfilled dream?

Why ask myself this question?

To remind myself that I do have a personal dream.

To ensure that I continue to work to my life's purpose.

To avoid living an unfulfilled life.

To check that my personal dream is aligned, or at least not in conflict, with my career dream.

Consider also questions: 57, 58, 78

What insights might I expect to gain?

Is that dream still the one that drives me? If not, why and what should I do?

Am I living my dream?

Is my dream about my work, career or my personal life, or is it a combination of both? Is there any conflict? Would disclosing my dream to others act as an additional spur to its fulfilment?

Is my dream unfulfilled because I am holding back for other reasons and, if so, what do I plan to do about them?

54. What is my worst nightmare?

Why ask myself this question?

I am really asking myself, "What would be the consequences if the worst thing I could imagine actually happened in my organisation?" This is a form of strategic scenario planning and the question is a powerful stimulus for risk-avoidance planning.

I can also question whether I am avoiding addressing the nightmare and its underlying causes for some reason, such as a personal or emotional relationship.

Consider also questions: 35, 46, 82

What insights might I expect to gain?

Risk is not just a nightmare scenario; I also have to think of probability and impact before I consider whether it is worth looking for a mitigating set of actions.

Thinking through my nightmare, and its causes, may help me to address it rationally rather than emotionally.

Learning both how to trust and to obey my 'gut' feelings.

55. How do I survive and flourish by changing faster than my environment?

Why ask myself this question?

My environment will change; anticipating and preparing for change reduces the subsequent pain of forced adaptation.

To avoid being an ostrich with my head in the sand – yesterday's person!

To question/understand the risks of remaining in my own comfort zone.

Embracing change should give me and my organisation an advantage.

Because the changes may be a threat or an opportunity.

The more change that I can anticipate, the less the associated risk.

Regularly considering this question results in both value protection and creation.

Consider also questions: 8, 56, 86

What insights might I expect to gain?

Gaining advantage from changes in my environment, though not all can be accurately forecast.

Learning more about changes and their likely impact.

Determining a process for divining significant change before it rises above the horizon and is also apparent to my competitors.

Identifying the significance of forecast change, both for my organisation and for me personally.

"Everyone seems busy, but nothing is getting done. Hiring more staff seems the only logical solution".

Notes

Notes

56. How do I learn?

Why ask myself this question?

There are many different ways of learning, both formal and informal; I must know and then choose what best suits my needs at any particular time.

"What got me here will not be certain to take me there", so do I understand how best I can be groomed – through my own efforts, too – for the most likely future I can envisage?

Unless I continue to learn, I'll never grow and my potential will be limited.

To appreciate that my preferred learning approaches are as important as the matters I will need to learn.

Consider also questions: 36, 59, 65

What insights might I expect to gain?

My willingness to place myself outside my comfort zone.

Whether I am stuck in my ways.

Whether I am frightened of anything new and, if so, why?

Whose opinions do I respect most? How can they help me to learn?

How I can ensure that my direct reports also value learning and continue their personal development?

When did I last learn or experience something new? What value did this have for me?

57. If I received a million dollars to persue my passion, what would I do?

Why ask myself this question?

This question is about how I view my life and aspirations.

To differentiate between principle and presumed predictability.

To discover how much I love my work.

Consider also questions: 20, 58, 73

References:
1. Hierarchy of Needs: http://www.maslow.com

What insights might I expect to gain?

Appreciating that lifestyle stages and maturity affect my decision-making.

Appreciating the value of understanding the relative importance of my job and my life.

Do I really need $1,000,000 to make the change?

Understanding where I am situated on Maslow's hierarchy of needs.

58. If I were guaranteed success, what would I attempt?
Why ask myself this question?

To question what I am able to do and what I would like to do.

Understanding risk will expand the field of possibilities.

How is it that exceptional individuals can achieve what appears to others to be impossible?

To uncover a fear that is holding me back.

Consider also questions: 32, 53, 79

What insights might I expect to gain?

Does hubris always need to be followed by nemesis?

Understanding my personal attitude to balancing risk and success.

Understanding how/why the horizons of what I might attempt are limited by fear of failure.

59. How am I doing, and how do I know?

Why ask myself this question?

My appraisal interview should offer me a golden opportunity to identify problems and opportunities, to increase my motivation and to improve my performance.

But often organisational leaders find themselves in a situation where they do not have a clear line manager, their line manager is not competent or is unuse to such appraisal processes. If this is the case, then I have to do my own appraisal, and do it well, because otherwise I will become increasingly disenchanted, baffled and alienated.

It is most useful for me to do a 360 degree review as this will help me understand the perceptions of my superior, peers and team. I should seek to understand perceptions rather than quantified performance metrics, as these will help me to understand how to respond and change behaviours.

Consider also questions: 36, 65, 69

What insights might I expect to gain?

How I believe I am doing may be very different from my colleagues' perception.

What measures I should choose for determining how I am doing. I must take my welfare into consideration, as well as my output.

Different perspectives on my performance will come from different stakeholders, but since there will be many goals I should sort out their hierarchy.

My goals may not be simply measurable but should still be explicable and I should discover how far others buy into my goals.

The feedback channels on achievement that should now be established. I should take care that the appraisal processes use people who relate to me directly in my work. Avoid any suggestion that my appraisals should be done by external consultants or by a remuneration committee.

"We can't wrap up this meeting yet. We've only been here for two hours."

Notes

Notes

60. What do I want from my team?

Why ask myself this question?

To determine what I have done to create clarity around personal purpose and interdependency.

To understand what the composition of my team should be.

If I don't understand what I want from my team, then I probably haven't got a team!

To enhance our shared enjoyment of working together.

What teams exist in my organisation? Are these teams formal or informal, temporary or relatively permanent?

Consider also questions: 43, 72, 99

What insights might I expect to gain?

Real leadership is about developing people through work.

Learning how differing expectations may be harnessed for the greater good.

As a leader, I should be developing leaders, as well as inspiring followers.

Gaining a deeper understanding of the members of my team.

Considering the value and outcomes of any team-building event.

Understanding how to balance short-term achievement with delivery of strategic goals.

Appreciating the value of a team culture.

The team of tomorrow, or some future day, is what I establish today.

61. Is there something not being said?

Why ask myself this question?

To identify the elephant in the room.

Because openness is essential for a team to work together.

To examine my own uneasiness.

We are what we tolerate.

Festering sores cause illness at times, even less convenient than now.

The silences are also important; we should listen for them.

To consider why 'the dog didn't bark in the night' – the culprit may be someone familiar!

Consider also questions: 4, 62, 71

What insights might I expect to gain?

Discover whom I trust.

What is being withheld?

Who are the holders of the secrets, why them and are they seeking to perpetuate their power base?

Getting to the bottom of this question may help to remove an impediment or foster advancement.

Understanding what might be the unintended consequences of any actions I take.

What would be the worst outcome if I chose to do nothing?

Whether or not my intuition is soundly based.

Ensuring that topics that make us uneasy are covered.

62. Who hasn't been heard on this issue?
Why ask myself this question?

To ensure that politeness and good practice have been exercised in polling the views and harnessing the experience and knowledge of all who might be able to advance action.

To garner the 'pride of authorship' that will aid implementation.

To foster contribution and to avoid alienation.

To elicit the good ideas.

Consider also questions: 36, 88, 93

What insights might I expect to gain?

The contributions and those who offer them will help me to develop the organisation's future capability while delivering on the required immediate actions.

Different perspectives can be illuminating.

Thinking about how to avoid paralysis by analysis.

Learning how to tie hearing to action through the contribution of all team members.

Ensuring that I am considered to be approachable.

63. What is my ideal outcome?

Why ask myself this question?

To articulate my ideal without first compromising.

To dare to dream.

There may be less than I imagined standing in the way of fulfilling my dream.

Because I lead and others may want to help me to fulfil my dream.

Dreams can seem fantastic but nevertheless can come true.

"The dreamers of the day are dangerous men, for they may act their dream with open eyes to make it possible."
T.E. Lawrence

Consider also questions: 20, 34, 58

What insights might I expect to gain?

Answering involves clarifying who I am.

Identifying who is involved in my outcome.

Testing and realising a dream is for a later stage; now the work is to dream.

Realism is not part of dreaming, so is my first answer too constrained?

Which part of me is dreaming?

The simplicity of an ideal outcome will make it easier to communicate and simpler to implement.

"Phew! I thought it was David with my annual performance review."

Notes

Notes

64. What is expected of me around here?

Why ask myself this question?

If I don't know the answer to this, then I may be concentrating on the wrong things.

I may have misunderstood. What should I be doing and who said so?

Meeting other's expectations is a key to success; the opposite is also true.

To ensure that I am, or am prepared to be, wholly behind the expectations others have of me.

To ensure that other team members (and all stakeholders) share the same expectations of me.

Because if it is to be, it is up to me.

Consider also questions: 1, 71, 82

What insights might I expect to gain?

What makes me ask this question right now?

Am I capable of and willing to meet expectations?

I may not like the answer to the question but it is better to know than not; I can then decide what to do next.

Will I need to reconcile the external expectations with my internal drivers and how will I do so?

What would I learn if I put this question directly to my superiors or my colleagues?

What are the alternatives?

"Good morning everyone! This is my new office spokesperson, his name is Scape: If you could direct any comments on my management style to him, that would be very much appreciated".

Notes

65. If I fail to perform, where do I go for help?

Why ask myself this question?

To be clear about my support system before I need to activate it.

To understand my weaknesses and how to address them.

To distinguish between my inherent weaknesses and other constraints upon my performance.

To appreciate better my position and, specifically, where danger lies and where help is available.

Consider also questions: 14, 36, 56

What insights might I expect to gain?

Do I have a support system I can trust?

In determining where help might be available, my thoughts will also be directed to the type of help I need.

However strong I may be as a leader, I will be even more effective in collaboration with others. Being willing and able to address my weaknesses is a sign of strength.

Have I identified sources of help ahead of any possible need? Should I seek their advice in advance of taking any action?

Exploring the possible causes of failure should help to avoid them in practice.

Discussing with others, especially chosen advisers, will be even more fruitful ahead of action rather than resorting to restitution afterwards.

How to make good even better.

66. Would I like to change the cast of players?

Why ask myself this question?

People matter most.

My choice of team members reveals my competence as a leader.

To ensure that the cast is appropriate for the task and that all the players are performing.

Is the existing cast likely to enhance or prejudice my reputation and that of the organisation?

Consider also questions: 12, 72, 92

References:

1. *Always change a winning team* Peter Robinson (Cyan Books and Marshall Cavendish, 2005)

What insights might I expect to gain?

What is providing me with a sense that change might be necessary?

What are my alternatives?

What the consequences may be if I choose to do nothing.

What would the impact be, elsewhere in the organisation and with external stakeholders, if I change my team?

An answer for the current situation could be very different from that for the future of the organisation.

The cast, if in place before my arrival in role, knows the history and the levers to pull for action. If I act prematurely, will I lose the 'essence' of the organisation as well as the goodwill of the 'survivors'?

67. Which unwritten rules are helping or hurting me?

Why ask myself this question?

To recognise the significance of relationships and the informal systems and learn how to use them.

If I don't know these rules, then I won't know if I'm breaking them or following them.

Because some of these may jeopardise my success.

Most successful organisations are open and seen to be so.

To eliminate, or at least reduce, the possibility of these rules impeding progress.

Consider also questions: 71, 82, 86

What insights might I expect to gain?

Discerning which levers are connected to which delivery mechanisms.

How to connect with, and harness, the real drivers of the organisation.

Appreciating that it is often the unwritten rules that form the basis of my organisation's culture and values.

Questioning if everything needs to be codified formally or if it would be helpful to permit the culture to develop informally to bind the team and aid progress.

Considering whether or not there would be value in making explicit what is now concealed so that all are able to understand and contribute to the best of their ability.

Understanding that all organisations have hidden networks and practices; too much forced exposure may prove destructive.

"He likes to keep the meetings short and to the point."

Notes

Notes

68. How do other people's perceptions of my power in the organisation affect the things I do?

Why ask myself this question?

To gain awareness of my influence – even when unintentional – on others in the organisation.

To understand the extent to which other people's opinions influence me.

Consider also questions: 4, 64, 69

What insights might I expect to gain?

Deciding how comfortable I am with my perceived power and how well I use/abuse it.

Reviewing if I have deliberately set out to achieve this level of power and, if not, do I know how to change it?

The formal power I wield in my organisation may be quite different from the informal power – one could be greater or less than the other. Do I know which is the case?

69. What perceptions that others have of me would I like to correct?

Why ask myself this question?

To discover how well I understand how others see me.

To create a benchmark for increasing my influence in my organisation.

To better understand myself.

Consider also questions: 36, 68, 77

What insights might I expect to gain?

Gaining a better understanding of other's perceptions based upon truth, not assumption.

Do I believe in myself? Am I confident enough to ask for frank feedback?

Requesting feedback is generally avoided unless absolutely necessary.

Being clear about other's perceptions will help me to correct them if necessary.

"Now that we're created fire, I'd like to discuss the creation of a 'Light and Heat Energy Distribution and Regulation Committee', of which naturally I would be the chairman. The first order of business I'd like to discuss is an increase in my salary and bonuses."

Notes

70. Why should my people be committed to my organisation?

Why ask myself this question?

To consider whether people know what they have to do and feel appreciated.

To review the degree to which my commitment is mirrored by my people.

Commitment is a two-way street: the organisation must commit for its people to commit.

Consider also questions: 26, 30, 81

What insights might I expect to gain?

Determining the various constituent elements of commitment: values, performance measures, strategic objectives, etc.

Discovering how both I and my organisation inspire – or could inspire – commitment from our people.

Understanding how committed I am to my organisation and to my work.

71. What do I tolerate round here that gets in the way?

Why ask myself this question?

To ensure that priority is given to managing the bottlenecks.

To ensure that sub-systems are not optimised at the expense of the whole organisation.

Better to have focused satisfaction than wasteful ineffectiveness.

To examine critically why I tolerate certain things.

Consider also questions: 67, 82, 86

What insights might I expect to gain?

Reviewing whether I am unusual in tolerating certain things or if others behave similarly.

Understanding better why I tolerate certain things and if these are damaging the organisation.

Deciding if I can do anything to change my and other's attitude and degree of toleration.

Notes

Notes

72. What do I do to encourage others to use their gifts?

Why ask myself this question?

To find out if I truly am a team player, or whether I just think of myself.

To consider if I support my colleagues and if I allow them to support me.

To understand whether I see the potential in my colleagues, or whether I wait for them to prove themselves before I believe in them.

A manager sees and organises competence; a leader sees the potential in people.

Consider also questions: 16, 43, 62

What insights might I expect to gain?

Determining how secure I feel and how satisfied I am with what I am doing.

I will not be able to help others use their gifts if I am insecure and dissatisfied.

Uncovering what is preventing me from helping others use their gifts.

Considering how well I know myself and how well do I know the needs of others and my organisation.

Reviewing how well I know my colleagues and their potential?

73. Are my priorities consistent with my purpose in life?

Why ask myself this question?

To ensure I am living my life as I wish in terms of goal, effort, pace and enjoyment of the outcomes.

To review whether my priorities and purpose in life have changed.

To question, continually, the process through which I examine my priorities.

Consider also questions: 53, 71, 78

What insights might I expect to gain?

Enquiring about my purpose in life enables me to keep it under review and analyse the cause of any changes.

By appraising my priorities, I am able, continually, to manage the way I live my life.

If I feel that I am achieving my purpose in life, then the confidence that results will reinforce the way I allocate my priorities and so establish a virtuous circle of gain.

Seeing if my priorities and purpose are in conflict in terms of work and personal life. If so, can I resolve such conflicts?

Reviewing, continually, the process through which I examine my priorities.

74. What are the likely future changes in my business landscape?

Why ask myself this question?

I may not have a crystal ball but this is no excuse for not looking into the future.

It is often unexpected changes in the environment that come to bite us, or to offer us opportunities that we frequently miss.

To develop a habit of stepping into a helicopter and taking a good look at what is happening in our world.

Anticipating change has many advantages: it reduces fear of the unknown; provides opportunities for value protection/creation; creates competitive advantage.

Consider also questions: 34, 38, 94

What insights might I expect to gain?

I may discover that my organisation has become too inward-looking.

I may be avoiding this because of the inevitable associated uncertainty. Dealing with change is child's play compared to coping with uncertainty.

How much time I spend navel-gazing.

Seeing what's on the horizon may allow us to take advantage of opportunities and protect us from potential threats.

Being alert to such changes better enables me and my organisation to adapt to them.

Determining if anticipated changes are short or long-term and if they apply to just my part of the organisation or to the whole.

"The quarterly profit figures were only supposed to blow your socks off."

© T. MCLELLAN

Notes

Notes

75. Is it time to change our winning strategy?
Why ask myself this question?

To recognise success and seek to replicate it rather than conduct post-mortems on what has not worked.

To avoid remaining in my/the organisation's comfort zone whilst the external environment is changing.

To understand better what other opportunities exist.

To determine what threats exist to our strategy.

Consider also questions: 5, 48, 55

What insights might I expect to gain?

Separating successful outcomes arising from luck or faulty reasoning, from well-reasoned thinking that uncontrollable factors then prevented from reaching fruition.

Identifying discernible patterns and strategies in our realised successful outcomes, the application of which could indicate future success earlier and with less risk.

Gaining greater knowledge of what works will boost the confidence that is required to differentiate ourselves from the competition.

Being careful not to apply strategies that have worked previously if the current circumstances and imperatives are different.

"Now that we've covered your 'HOW TO EAT AN ELEPHANT' strategic planning philosophy, I thought you might want to start applying it."

Notes

Notes

76. What no longer works for me?

Why ask myself this question?

To stop and assess my situation. Sometimes we are so caught up with putting out fires that we lose sight of fulfilling our purpose.

To understand that what no longer works for me provides a choice: that of continuing as is, or taking action and changing what no longer works for me.

Consider also questions: 53, 78, 84

What insights might I expect to gain?

Realising that I may have to confront my fears. I may be tolerating what no longer works because it's the easy option.

Knowing how to avoid life passing me by.

Understanding how to take control of my life, both at work and home.

77. What do I really want from my relationships?

Why ask myself this question?

Work and personal life is built around relationships; understanding these better will help to build more satisfaction in both aspects of my life.

To distinguish between what I 'want' and what I would 'like' to have from my relationships.

To understand better the need to give and take in any relationship.

To reflect upon my personal needs and those of others.

Consider also questions: 59, 61, 99

What insights might I expect to gain?

Understanding how important a relationship is to me.

Understanding how attached I am to my opinions – to being right, to my point of view.

Realising the opportunity to build closer and deeper relationships, both at work and home.

Understanding better my own needs and how others may help me – and vice versa.

Where to go for help if needed.

78. How much longer before I can live the life I want to but haven't because of all the things I've had to do?

Why ask myself this question?

To understand better why I feel unfulfilled, unhappy, frustrated.

To re-organise my priorities in life.

As long as I am busy, I don't have to face life's tough questions. Am I sticking my head in the sand and, if so, why?

None of us leads a perfect life but we can always aim to get closer to doing so. I am unlikely to succeed, or be fulfilled, in anything that I do if I leave this question unanswered.

Life is not a dress rehearsal.

Consider also questions: 42, 73, 86

What insights might I expect to gain?

Understanding what I want from life and how I am going to achieve it before it's too late.

Realising what I have to:
- stop doing
- start doing
- do more consistently.

Uncovering whose consent or help I need to achieve this and how to obtain it.

Analysing what kind of life I want to live, what things are really important to me and what is preventing me from living as I want.

Understanding what it would take for me to feel in control of my own destiny, whether I am frightened of taking control and why.

Analysing if I am giving the important things in my life the right priorities?

Thinking about whether others have ever commented that I'm in the wrong job or career.

79. If I could invest £100K to promote competitiveness, what would I spend it on?

Why ask myself this question?

To understand what makes my organisation competitive now and might/likely to in the future.

To see where I could make a contribution/suggestion to/for my organisation's competitiveness.

To focus myself on the need for my organisation to remain competitive.

Consider also questions: 47, 74, 81

What insights might I expect to gain?

Understanding better what makes my organisation competitive and how I can contribute to that both now and in the future.

Appreciating what difference a limited investment might make and focusing my mind on that opportunity.

Checking if I am aligned with my organisation's ambitions, strategy and objectives.

I can make a better decision about what might make a competitive difference by considering the answer to this question.

How well did I spot the impact of social media on my organisation?

"Thank you everyone for being here on a Saturday to discuss time efficiency in company meetings. Now that we've been here all day, I'd like to analyse today's session, and infact if we needed to be here today at all."

Notes

Notes

80. What are my frustrations and disappointments?

Why ask myself this question?

To consider, before taking action, what has failed in the past and to minimise the potential for its re-occurrence for myself and my organisation.

20/20 hindsight is relatively easy, but it can also help foresight and improve decision-making.

To learn from my mistakes.

To understand why these occurred.

Consider also questions: 71, 77, 82

What insights might I expect to gain?

Understanding what is in my control and what is outside it in order that I can balance opportunity and risk.

Learning from my mistakes and those of my organisation.

Understanding the reasons for my frustrations and disappointments.

Avoiding dwelling on the past while learning from it to build a more positive future.

81. What attracts customers and employees to my organisation?

Why ask myself this question?

To understand why I work for my organisation and if I am aligned with its purpose and values.

To understand both my organisation's customers and employees better – without them, my organisation would fail.

To perform more effectively with regard to both customers and employees.

Consider also questions: 15, 26, 98

What insights might I expect to gain?

Realising that rapid change, internal or external, may undermine these critical stakeholder strengths.

Considering how to build on these strengths.

Understanding better my organisation's competitive advantages, both in terms of employees and customers.

82. What am I pretending not to know or to see?

Why ask myself this question?

To acknowledge the presence of rocks and icebergs and steer accordingly.

To ensure that I am as intellectually honest as I would like my team to be.

To deal with demons rather than permit their devilment.

To identify whom I can find to deal with the matters I have chosen not to remedy.

Consider also questions: 4, 61, 75

What insights might I expect to gain?

Understanding what benefit and what detriment may result from this behaviour.

Finding ways of positively changing my attitude and behaviour.

Accepting that my behaviour can influence my team's behaviour.

Acknowledging that I don't want to be what I tolerate.

83. What decision am I avoiding?

Why ask myself this question?

To avoid decisions being taken by others and not necessarily in my best interests.

To ensure that I am in control of my destiny.

To seek help in facing the decision and possibly share the taking of it.

Consider also questions: 32, 88, 93

What insights might I expect to gain?

Understanding what I fear in relation to these decisions.

Appreciating that not all my decisions have to be proved right.

Knowing who might help me in reaching a decision.

"Quickly!! Sign it before you start thinking logically."

Notes

Notes

84. What's working well for me at the moment?

Why ask myself this question?

To try to build on my strengths and minimise my weaknesses.

To count my blessings and be grateful for what I have; to see the glass half-full.

To focus on continuous improvement.

To take stock, regularly.

To compare outcomes against the previously agreed goals.

To replicate my success.

Consider also questions: 48, 59, 87

What insights might I expect to gain?

Knowing why things are working well and whether it is because of serendipity or deliberate decisions on my part.

Understanding how I can sustain this situation.

Evaluating what is coming over the horizon that might impact my success.

85. How much time do I spend working on my business and how much working in it?

Why ask myself this question?

As I am both the leader of an organisation and its manager, I must be aware that this can result in loss of productivity, cause waste, and may even lead to failure. There are at least five sources of conflict I need to consider.

Choice of effort – The more work is done as a manager, the less the contribution to profitability as the focus is too narrow.

Perquisite taking – Leaders tend to be overpaid while lower-level employees are underpaid thus resulting in a conflict between all involved.

Differential risk exposure – Leaders typically have substantial levels of human capital and personal wealth invested in the firm which makes them excessively risk-averse.

Differential horizons – Leaders want their profits while managers only want to work and make enough to keep their pockets full.

Over investment – Managers tend to empire-build whilst leaders will pursue profits.

Consider also questions: 27, 41, 73

What insights might I expect to gain?

Learning to see the wood for the trees.

Working 'on' my organisation allows me to take a step up, to have a bird's eye view, and to better strategise and plan.

Understanding better how to manage my conflicting roles as the leader and manager of my organisation.

Redressing any imbalances between my work and my life.

86. What's getting in the way of me getting things done and reaching my and the organisation's potential?

Why ask myself this question?

To ensure that priority is given to managing the bottlenecks.

To ensure that sub-systems are not optimised at the expense of the whole organisation.

Consider also questions: 8, 34, 80

What insights might I expect to gain?

Finding the root causes of any disconnects in the way I work.

Analysing if what I do is aligned with my organisation's strategy and strengths.

Discovering if I am in the right role in my organisation.

87. What is my unique contribution?
Why ask myself this question?

To better understand my value.

To understand how I can get ahead and stay ahead of my competitors, both corporate and personal.

So I can focus my efforts and develop a unique level of expertise in areas that really matter to my customers and organisation and because of this, I'll command the rewards that come with this expertise.

So I can develop the skills and abilities that my organisation most values, win respect and get the career advancement that I want.

Consider also questions: 37, 87, 86

What insights might I expect to gain?

Understanding my own strengths and weaknesses.

Knowing my strengths is important to build and develop them.

Knowing what really works and plan for more; knowing what does not work and eliminate it.

Checking if this is the contribution expected of me.

Understanding to what part of the process or outcome it contributes.

"I've removed the hands from all the clocks in this conference room, as today's meeting will be infinite. — We'll stop halfway through for lunch!"

Notes

Notes

88. How do I encourage constructive dissent in my organisation?

Why ask myself this question?

'Creative friction' leads to innovation – the ultimate competitive edge.

To consider if there is enough trust in my organisation for open discussions to take place.

To ensure I do not surround myself with 'yes people'.

Consider also questions: 56, 62, 72

What insights might I expect to gain?

Examining what culture I am fostering in my organisation.

Reviewing how safe people feel in speaking up.

Understanding what I can do to encourage discussion.

Ensuring that apparent harmony does not drive out productive conflict.

"Thank you, Miss Adams, great idea,
Shall I ask one of the men to suggest it?""

Notes

Notes

89. How do I respond to diversity issues?

Why ask myself this question?

To understand better what influences my behaviour and thereby gain greater objectivity.

To appreciate better the different types of diversity.

To ensure that my organisation benefits from the widest possible thinking from diverse sources.

Consider also questions: 37, 67, 90

What insights might I expect to gain?

Understanding better whether or not I bring any prejudice to bear on my treatment of others.

Testing my own degree of open-mindedness to different views and opinions.

Realising that my own reaction is not the only one possible.

Knowing how to facilitate open discussion.

90. What do I do to embed our values and ethics?
Why ask myself this question?

To check if I am at ease with my organisation's values and ethics.

To understand whether or not my organisation's values and ethics are 'real' or just 'words' – and just how seriously they are taken.

To test the degree to which they have been accepted by everyone and are practised by default.

To become a player, not just an observer.

Consider also questions: 1, 7, 99

What insights might I expect to gain?

Examining if I understand and know our values and ethics, and agree with them.

Checking if it came naturally to me to embed them by my actions.

Reviewing if I treat this initiative as part of my leadership role with those who look to me to set an example.

If the values and ethics are not taken seriously, asking myself if this is an organisation for which I want to work.

If they are taken seriously, asking myself if my own personal values are aligned.

Understanding what is important to me in terms of the organisation for which I work.

Reviewing my role in modelling values and ethics.

91. How often do I say 'No' and how do I say it?

Why ask myself this question?

To know what's really important to me and why – it's easier always to say 'Yes'.

To understand truly why I say 'Yes' or 'No'.

To understand that saying 'No' is as important as saying 'Yes'.

Am I able to say 'No' without justifying myself? If not, do I know why I need to provide justification? Could it not be that I simply chose to say 'No'?

Consider also questions: 82, 83, 88

What insights might I expect to gain?

Understanding why I may be afraid of saying 'No'.

Appreciating the risks of always being seen as either a 'Yes' or a 'No' person.

Analysing whether I say 'No' to processes or outcomes, or both.

Examining if I am able to say 'No' without justifying myself and, if not, knowing why I need to provide justification.

Checking if I always give clear reasons for saying 'No'.

92. What aspects of the culture of my organisation attract customers?

Why ask myself this question?

To learn what attracts and retains loyal customers and what to do to reinforce it.

To enhance the long-term viability of the business.

To check if I understand the culture of my organisation and how this is perceived and valued externally.

For all to understand that the organisation exists only to serve the needs of its customers.

To focus enquiry on the way we work on the aspects that bring advantage to existing customers and serve to attract new ones.

Consider also questions: 37, 45, 96

What insights might I expect to gain?

Knowing what to do to attract and retain loyal customers.

Prioritising what customers believe to be important.

Analysing how well I know my customers and how well they know me and my organisation.

Understanding what has no perceived benefit for customers: marking it for query and probable elimination because it will absorb resource for no benefit.

Thinking on this issue will also enable my team to be heard on the aspects of the organisation's culture that impact on their roles.

93. Whom do I consult before taking difficult decisions?

Why ask myself this question?

When I am considering how to make better business decisions, it helps me to have a way of talking about the available options. There are four common ways of making decisions: command, consult, vote and consensus. These four options represent increasing degrees of involvement. Increased involvement brings the benefit of increased commitment along with the curse of decreased decision-making efficiency.

If my team is strong and I have great relationships, I can make many decisions by turning the final choice over to someone I trust to make a good decision. Consulting is a process whereby decision-makers invite others to influence them before they make their choice. You can consult with experts, a representative population, or even everyone who wants to offer an opinion.

The important thing about consultation is, however, that I retain the right, having listened, to make the decision.

Consider also questions: 11, 33, 44

What insights might I expect to gain?

Helps to isolate conflicts and trade-offs which are making it a difficult decision.

Identifying who would be my 'phone a friend' on different decisions.

Understanding better my role in the organisation.

Identifying gaps in my own competences and knowledge.

94. How can I measure the resilience of my organisation?

Why ask myself this question?

To provide me with a quantitative snapshot of my organisation's resilience and to identify its resilience strengths and weaknesses.

To understand how resilience varies across my organisation and to investigate my organisation's crisis memory – have lessons really been learnt from past crises?

To provide me with intelligence to feed into decisions about how I can improve my organisational resilience.

To prepare my organisation for future change.

Consider also questions: 9, 55, 56

References:

1. Managing at the Speed of Change by Daryl R Connor (Wiley & Sons, 1997) http://www.davidmays.org/BN/ConMana.html

What insights might I expect to gain?

Understanding the different elements of resilience.

Reviewing if my organisation's resilience is increasing or decreasing – and why.

Analysing how my organisation has reacted to the last major change in its markets and how this differed from its competitors.

95. What is my predecessor's legacy?

Why ask myself this question?

I should understand what my predecessor has left behind so I can continue to build on the positive facets of his legacy in the future.

How connected was he with who he is and what he represents as an individual and a leader?

Did he have a solid identity and a set of values which were translated into a set of guiding principles?

Did he trust his gut and was he courageous enough to take calculated risks?

Did he inspire happiness in those who supported his leadership?

Was he incredibly self-disciplined and held himself accountable for consistently delivering to his standards every day?

Consider also questions: 13, 22, 66

What insights might I expect to gain?

Realising that I may have only a short time before my predecessor's problems become mine.

Differentiating between what I see as benefits and impediments of this legacy.

Knowing whether or not to reinforce this legacy.

Understanding the impact of the legacy on others.

96. What would my greatest competitor say about me?

Why ask myself this question?

To raise competitor awareness and to uncover how well I know our customers.

To see my organisation from my competitors' and my customers' points of view.

To celebrate achievements – our competitive edge – and to identify performance gaps.

To provide an input to business strategy.

Consider also questions: 15, 31, 70

What insights might I expect to gain?

Discovering if I am better, or worse, than I had thought.

Prompting new strategic initiatives.

Learning something new about my competitors and about my organisation.

"It's just a little thing I like to do to relieve stress after a long week at work."

Notes

Notes

97. How do I balance 'work' and 'life'?

Why ask myself this question?

Life and work are said to be the cornerstones of being human and both are very important for happiness. Yet juggling the demands of each can be difficult. By thinking differently, I can perhaps find ways to have a better balance between work and home.

To keep asking the question before it's too late.

To resolve any imbalance.

To take control of my life and destiny.

To prove to others that I care about this issue.

Consider also questions: 40, 73, 78

What insights might I expect to gain?

Identifying what is important to me, both in 'life' and 'work'.

Reviewing my priorities in terms of both.

Identifying what makes me feel fulfilled in both.

Checking if my priorities changed over time and are likely to change again in the future.

Reviewing whose views I need to consider as I contemplate changes for myself.

Examining if I can distinguish between work and life.

98. How do I learn about my customers' needs?

Why ask myself this question?

Understanding my customers is the key to giving them good service. To give good customer care, I must deliver what I promise. But customer care involves getting to know my customers so well that I can anticipate their needs and exceed their expectations.

To understand my customers well, I need to be attentive to them whenever I am in contact with them.

There are three main ways to understand my customers better. One is to put myself in their shoes and try and look at my organisation from their point of view. The second way is to collect and analyse data in order to shed light on their buying behaviour. The third way is simply to ask them what they think.

Consider also questions: 11, 45, 92

What insights might I expect to gain?

The potential rewards are great: I can increase customer loyalty and bring in new business through positive word-of-mouth recommendation.

Understanding the process, or lack thereof, whereby my organisation captures and uses information on customer needs.

Identifying what I must do to learn more about my customers.

99. Do I ask my team how my actions make them feel?
Why ask myself this question?

Asking for – and giving – honest feedback is one of the most difficult things to do, yet it is also one of the most powerful ways of building trust.

If I have a cohesive team, both I and the team will work better.

Asking for feedback and acting upon it, will demonstrate that I care about my team and build cohesiveness. It will also help us learn from each other.

By surfacing and dealing with any issues that arise, my team will almost certainly perform better.

Consider also questions: 36, 60, 77

What insights might I expect to gain?

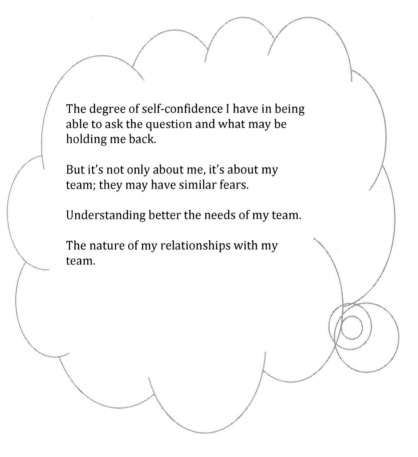

The degree of self-confidence I have in being able to ask the question and what may be holding me back.

But it's not only about me, it's about my team; they may have similar fears.

Understanding better the needs of my team.

The nature of my relationships with my team.

The 99 Questions

1. Are my values aligned with those practised in my organisation?
2. How do I measure success?
3. Do I understand why the people at the top are in their positions'
4. What would I prefer that others did not know?
5. What do I see over the horizon that others have not seen?
6. What is the most searching question I could ask now?
7. What do I do when the behaviour of others clashes with policies procedures or culture?
8. What are the current constraints on growth?
9. How adaptable is my organisation?
10. What proportion of my staff can explain our business model?
11. Who are my five key stakeholders?
12. Is the spread of length of service of my senior team appropriate
13. Why does my organisation need a goal other than survival?
14. Who is really my boss?
15. What is the unique competence of my organisation?
16. How do I ensure the welfare of my team?
17. How can I ensure that everyone understands the profit and loss statement?
18. What is the first thing I could do to improve cash flow?
19. How would my people know I love them?
20. What would I like my legacy to be?
21. How do I know I am being told the truth?
22. Which three adjectives would I use to describe both success and failure in my organisation?

23. Do I need more external advice?

24. Could I use a mentor or coach?

25. Which organisation do I most admire?

26. What astonishes me most about my organisation?

27. Do I take all my annual leave?

28. When on holiday, how often do I access my emails?

29. I am in a coffee shop and start talking to a stranger. I am asked what my organisation does. Can I answer this in 30 seconds such that the stranger says 'tell me more'?

30. Why am I proud of the organisation for which I work?

31. What would the world be like without my organisation?

32. If I were the sole owner of my organisation, what one thing would I change?

33. Who are the influencers in my organisation?

34. Imagine that consultants have fairy dust that they can sprinkle over your organisation to change it in any way you want. What would you like it to do for yours?

35. When something goes wrong, how do I know if it's important?

36. What do I do to demonstrate that I take feedback seriously?

37. How do my actions support the culture of my organisation?

38. How does innovation happen in my organisation?

39. What are the first three things I would suggest my successor reviews?

40. What would be the consequences if I took three months off?

41. Am I a workaholic or do I just love my job?

42. What would cause me to consider leaving my job or changing careers?

43. How much time do I allow my people for training and personal development?

44. How do I encourage value from our non-executives?

45. How should I target the 'right' customers, internal and external?

46. To which uncertainty affecting my organisation would I most like the answer?

47. Looking back from three years into the future, what three things did we do to achieve the success we had planned?

48. Looking back from three years into the future, everything has gone terribly for our organisation. What did I fail to do?

49. What one thing could the Government do that would help us to succeed?

50. I am now Chief Executive of my organisation: what two things will I do immediately?

51. How would I brief a person who is replacing me for a few months about this 'issue'?

52. How do I set, use and communicate priorities?

53. What is my unfulfilled dream?

54. What is my worst nightmare?

55. How do I survive and flourish by changing faster than my environment?

56. How do I learn?

57. If I received a million dollars to pursue my passion, what would I do?

58. If I were guaranteed success, what would I attempt?

59. How am I doing, and how do I know?

60. What do I want from my team?

61. Is there something not being said?

62. Who hasn't been heard on this issue?

63. What is my ideal outcome?

64. What is expected of me around here?

65. If I fail to perform, where do I go for help?

66. Would I like to change the cast of players?

67. Which unwritten rules are helping or hurting me?

68. How do other people's perceptions of my power in the organisation affect the things I do?

69. What perceptions that others have of me would I like to correct?

70. Why should my people be committed to my organisation?

71. What do I tolerate round here that gets in the way?

72. What do I do to encourage others to use their gifts?

73. Are my priorities consistent with my purpose in life?

74. What are the likely future changes in my business landscape?

75. Is it time to change our winning strategy?

76. What no longer works for me?

77. What do I really want from my relationships?

78. How much longer before I can live the life I want to but haven't because of all the things I've had to do?

79. If I could invest £100K to promote competitiveness, what would I spend it on?

80. What are my frustrations and disappointments?

81. What attracts customers and employees to my organisation?

82. What am I pretending not to know or to see?

83. What decision am I avoiding?

84. What's working well for me at the moment?

85. How much time do I spend working on my business and how much working in it?

86. What's getting in the way of me getting things done and reaching my and the organisation's potential?

87. What is my unique contribution?

88. How do I encourage constructive dissent in my organisation?

89. How do I respond to diversity issues?

90. What do I do to embed our values and ethics?

91. How often do I say 'No' and how do I say it?

92. What aspects of the culture of my organisation attract customers?

93. Whom do I consult before taking difficult decisions?

94. How can I measure the resilience of my organisation?

95. What is my predecessor's legacy?

96. What would my greatest competitor say about me?

97. How do I balance 'work' and 'life'?

98. How do I learn about my customers' needs?

99. Do I ask my team how my actions make them feel?

Appendix – Origins of this book

The authors are all members of the Worshipful Company of Management Consultants (www.wcomc.org), a livery company in the City of London. Though having diverse professional disciplines to support their practice as consultants, they all enjoy conviviality and giving free rein to their sense of curiosity.

At one company event, they considered the questions that they had found most useful in gaining an understanding of their clients' problems. They agreed that the most appropriate questions could lead more surely to sound thinking and robust plans than the superficially-attractive answers that their clients often employed. From that realisation, they refined a list of questions that covered some of the more common situations that their clients had encountered in working with others and in developing leadership skills. This book is the outcome of their debate.

The authors hope that you will find the questions helpful in your situations and would welcome any feedback via their website:

www.99essentialquestions.com

Lightning Source UK Ltd.
Milton Keynes UK
UKOW03f136121216

289779UK00002B/513/P